GHIBERTI

COMPLETE EDITION

PHAIDON

KING SOLOMON AND THE QUEEN OF SHEBA

BRONZE RELIEF
ON GHIBERTI'S SECOND DOOR
AFTER THE RECENT CLEANING
FLORENCE BAPTISTERY

GHIBERTI

BY LUDWIG GOLDSCHEIDER

PHAIDON PUBLISHERS INC
DISTRIBUTED BY OXFORD UNIVERSITY PRESS NEW YORK

FIRST EDITION: 1949
MADE IN GREAT BRITAIN
PRINTED BY CLARKE & SHERWELL LTD · NORTHAMPTON

LIST OF CONTENTS

Fig. 1.   Detail from Solomon and the Queen of Sheba.
Bronze Relief, after cleaning (cf. plate 71)

FOREWORD

THE PRELIMINARY WORK in connection with this book had been completed by 1939 and the plates—with few exceptions—were printed in 1943, but, for reasons which there is no point in recalling here, the publication of the book has been postponed for several years. Most of the photographs were taken before the two doors had been cleaned and before they glistened with their old gilding as they do now. As can be seen from the few reproductions in this volume made after the latest cleaning, Ghiberti's picturesque reliefs were more effective in photographs when patina and dirt filled the hollows and only the most prominent portions caught the light. "Ghiberti," says Rumohr, "frequently allowed his figures to dissolve into a picturesque mellowness, as in the beautiful, and beautifully turned, angels on the reliquary sarcophagus in Florence Cathedral, whose bodies are merged with the long, flowing draperies, thus emphasizing their derivation from Florentine painting of the period." Although the reliefs, especially those of the "Gate of Paradise", have gained from the cleaning as regards clarity of details, at the same time they have lost their rich gradation of tones and no longer show the mellowing influence of time, on which artists so often rely when they create their works.

The coloured frontispiece is after a photograph by Brogi di Laurati; Figures 22 and 29 and Plate 3-A are after photographs for which I am indebted to Professor Filippo Rossi of the Museo Nazionale in Florence, who has also given me much valuable advice. Dr. Lamberto Donati of Rome provided the original for Figure 7 and Professor F. Novotny of Vienna that for Plate 128. Plates 120, 125 and 127 have been reproduced from official museum photographs, for the use of which I have to thank the respective directors. Plates 126 and 133 to 141 are after new photographs by Laurati; the nine windows in Florence Cathedral were very carefully photographed after the cleaning and are here reproduced for the first time. Plates 2, 4, 22-26, 73, 112-A, 112-B, 122-124 and 129-132 are based on old photographs by Alinari, Brogi and others. All the remaining photographs for this volume were specially made by I. Schneider-Lengyel of Paris.

Of the fifty odd works which in the course of years have, with much optimism but little reason, been attributed to Ghiberti, I have reproduced only very few (in the Notes on the Plates). Of the others I have given a list, with references to catalogues and books in which reproductions of them may be found.

The text of Ghiberti's autobiography has here been translated into English for the first time and for great assistance in this connection I am indebted to the painter and sculptor Adrian Allinson. The quotations from Baldinucci were translated by Dr. I. Grafe. Vasari's "Vita" of Ghiberti is reproduced, by kind permission of Messrs. J. M. Dent and Sons, from the Everyman's Library edition, the annotations being by myself. Mr. R. H. Boothroyd has helped me with the English version of the Introduction. Sir Eric Maclagan and Mr. John Pope-Hennessy have given generous counsel. I am obliged to the directors of libraries in Florence and elsewhere for information and the loan of printed works.

London, March 1949   L.G.

Fig. 2. Weasel hunting a bird. Detail from the frame of Ghiberti's
first Baptistery Door

INTRODUCTION

I

" Let it always be remembered that life is short, that knowledge is endless, and that many doubts deserve not to be cleared."
Samuel Johnson, 1760

THE BAPTISTERY OF FLORENCE, San Giovanni, an octagonal, black-and-white building, the cupola of which is hidden beneath a pyramidal roof, stands opposite the Campanile and the Cathedral, both of which are of much more recent date. Nowadays the rattle of passing trams makes it difficult to contemplate undisturbed the three bronze doors, and it is even more difficult to carry one's mind back to those days of the late Middle Ages when the doors were still new to the eyes of the Florentines. The main door, facing the Cathedral, with its ten compartments of reliefs representing stories from the Old Testament, is Lorenzo Ghiberti's masterpiece. The two side-doors, each of which has twenty-eight compartments in Gothic quatrefoils, form a pair, despite the fact that they are not by the same master. The door with episodes from the New Testament is a youthful work of Ghiberti's; the other, showing scenes from the life of John the Baptist, was created a hundred years earlier by Andrea Pisano.

Boccaccio tells us in one of his " Novelle " what the Baptistery looked like about the year 1300, when it had only one wooden door instead of the three bronze doors : " One day it befell so that Guido Cavalcanti came, as was not seldom his wont, from Or San Michele by the Corso degli Adimari as far as San Giovanni, around which were then the antique great marble sarcophagi, of which many are today in the Cathedral, while some, and not a few, are around the Baptistery; and so Guido stood between the columns of porphyry, that are there, and the sarcophagi and the door of San Giovanni."

In 1439, when the Baptistery had already two of its doors and the third was almost finished, the Moor Pero Tafur passed through Florence, but all he had to say about it was : " There is a great square in front of the Cathedral, and in the centre is a very great church, worked with mosaics within and covered with lead without. They call it San Giovanni Battista." Not a word about Ghiberti's bronze doors, which at that time were already famous and were praised by all who wrote about art in Italy during the following two centuries. In 1436, when Leon Battista Alberti wanted to give Brunelleschi a list of great contemporary masters, he wrote : " Since my return to my own country after a long exile, I have perceived that in many, and above all in thee, Philippo, and in our dear friend Donatello the sculptor, and in those others, Ghiberti, Luca della Robbia and Masaccio, there dwells a spirit which is capable of the highest things and which is in no wise inferior to that of the great antique masters, great and famous though they may have been in art." And the Florentine art historians from Vasari (1550) to Baldinucci (1681) all included Ghiberti among the great masters.

Even before Baldinucci, an Englishman, Richard Lassels, who went to Florence in 1635, found words of praise for Ghiberti : " Near to the *Duomo* stands the Baptistery or round church of St John, where all the Children of the Town are baptized. The Brazen Doors of it (three in all) are admirable, especially that which looks towards the Great Church . . . These Doors are all of Brass historied into figures, containing the remarkable Histories of both the Testaments. They were

(9)

the work of brave Laurentius Cion, who spent fifty Years in making them : a long time, I confess ; but this is what Apelles called *aeternitati pingere*, to work things that will outlast Brass, and be famous for ever."

In the eighteenth century Ghiberti was still not appreciated in France and Germany, but in England he found recognition. In 1773 Thomas Patch, who was Reynolds's travelling companion in Italy, published in Florence his book of copperplate engravings of the bronze doors, and in 1780, when the Royal Academy moved to Somerset House, the library was decorated with casts from the reliefs of the *Gate of Paradise*, "the first works of the Quattrocento to find general acceptance in England".

Artistic Frenchmen who visited Florence during the eighteenth century had other ideas and either took no notice of Ghiberti or treated him in cavalier fashion. The most important of them, Charles de Brosse, wrote in 1739 to M. de Quintin : "Opposite the Cathedral is a former Temple of Mars, of octagonal form, which has been converted into a Baptistery. It has four bronze doors, on which scenes out of the Old Testament are wrought in small compartments. Michelangelo is reported to have thought these worthy of being the Gates of Paradise : this is not the only foolish remark that is accredited to him. Be it as it may, if those who admire these gates had seen the gates of the Chateau de Maisons near St Germain, I think they would prefer the latter."

De Brosse did not even take the trouble to count the doors or to look at the scenes represented thereon ; he did not like them. On the other hand, they made a very deep impression on another Frenchman who came to Florence more than a hundred years later. Hippolyte Taine wrote of them : "Sculpture, which with Nicola Pisano had already equalled painting, surpassed it in the fifteenth century, and the doors of the Baptistery show us with what sudden perfection and with what an impulse that occurred . . . Ghiberti was passionately fond of the antique. From Greece he caused torsos, heads and vases to be sent to him, which he completed, copied and admired. 'It is impossible,' he says in his *Commentarii*, 'to express in words the perfection of an antique statue ; it has infinite delicacies which the eye alone cannot grasp, but which only the hands can discover by feeling . . .' A man who has such a vivid perception of classical perfection is not far from achieving it himself . . . About 1400 Ghiberti was commissioned to create the two doors, and in his hands we see pure Greek beauty resurrected. In his reliefs there are innumerable female figures which in the nobility of their heads and bodies, in the simplicity and the quiet lines of their pose, produce the same effect as Athenian masterpieces . . . Processions uncoil and wind as if around a vase. Figures and groups counterbalance each other and take up positions as in a Greek chorus, and the harmonious forms of Greek architecture enframe in pillared halls the earnest figures, the graceful sweep of the draperies, the varied, elegant and restrained attitudes of the bodies, as in the performance of an antique tragedy. There is one young warrior who looks like Alcibiades ; in front of him there strides a Roman consul, while graceful young women half turn to watch and raise one arm. One of them is like a Juno, another like an Amazon, all are caught in one of those rare moments when the nobility of corporeal life attains its full perfection without effort and without deliberation . . . No artist except Raphael

View of Florence, about 1380, with the Baptistery in the centre. Detail of the Madonna della Misericordia at the Bigallo, Florence

has rendered more happily that precious moment of measure and moderation, of natural and exquisite invention. The *School of Athens* and the *Loggie* in the Vatican seem to derive from the same school as the door of the Baptistery, and to heighten the similarity still more, Ghiberti treats his bronze like a painter ; with their abundance of figures, the significance of their landscapes, the use of perspective, the diversity and gradation of the backgrounds merging with one another, which recede and lead the eye into depth, Ghiberti's reliefs become paintings."

With Taine's description the story of Ghiberti's fame reaches its climax ; no later writer has excelled it. Dvořák (1919) again drew attention to the relationship to Raphael ; Schlosser refers in general terms to the beauty, charm and classical perfection of Ghiberti's masterpiece. Other writers, e.g., Schmarsow and Lionello Venturi, have stressed the marked Gothic element which survives in Ghiberti's work, without mentioning that this is only the case when he is following the style prevalent in his time, and not his own new, pioneer ideas.

Ghiberti's return to a classical style had little influence on the formative arts in the nineteenth century, which instead took Raphael as their model. But when the Pre-Raphaelites tried to go back beyond Raphael and, in one of their first meetings in autumn 1848, compiled a " list of immortal thinkers and workers "—a list which begins with Jesus Christ and the author of the Book of Job—Dante Gabriel Rossetti inserted the names of three sculptors—Phidias, Michelangelo, Ghiberti.

II

" Non vide me' di me chi vide il vero . . ."
" Who saw the real, did not see better than I . . ."
Purgatorio, XII, 68

TAINE was quite right in remarking that Ghiberti's reliefs (at all events those on his second door) are paintings rather than works of sculpture. They achieve their effect through the play of light and shadow, not by means of line and form ; they have not only linear, but also aerial perspective—the eye does not encounter a rigid background, on which the swellings and hollows of flat sculpture stand, but, as in an illusionistic painting, is led into depth, into an endless atmosphere, where the light is caught by the tops of the ridges, and shadows without definite outlines gather in the hollows. Rumohr (1830) expressed this in his own way when he wrote : " In general these doors . . . in their treatment of form and movement, are so completely unique and inimitable that in them the spirit of painting has expressed itself through the medium of sculpture—exquisitely from the point of view of painting, and adequately from that of sculpture, and in any case in no wise unpleasing. They must be regarded as paintings and not as works of sculpture, if we wish to grasp their whole value and significance, instead of merely enjoying them. They look like paintings when we see them illuminated by the oblique rays of a bright morning sun, and it was as paintings that the artist, unhampered by the demands of sculptural style, conceived them." In this respect Ghiberti reveals his derivation from the antique art of Italy, for the art of the Renaissance was a return to the spatial illusion of the antique. We need only read Wickhoff's description of a Roman relief on the arch of Titus, in order to understand that Ghiberti was not thereby violating the laws of sculpture, but was returning to the old laws : " The depths of the relief exhibit a subtle variation from the full figures of the front plane to the flatly worked heads of the lowest layer on their vanishing backgrounds . . . the swellings and sinkings of the surface are various and depend only on the effect of the illusion, which is intended, but not on definite levels . . . Sculpture attempts here to achieve by its own means what highly developed painting attains—the impression of complete illusion . . . Air, light and shade must all help to produce the deceptive appearance of reality. The relief has *respirazione* (breath, atmosphere), like pictures by Velázquez."

Ghiberti's style is analysed by Bertha Friedmann, Hedwig Gollob, August Schmarsow, Paul Schubring, Lionello Venturi and Adrian Stokes—without much profit.

For the sake of exactitude and in order to be quite comprehensible, we ought here to investigate to what extent the realism and naturalism of Italian plastic art has been preserved throughout the centuries, for example, in the death-masks, which run from Julius Caesar to Lorenzo de' Medici ; we would have to ask ourselves when the abstract expressionistic style had to start defending itself against the realistic-illusionistic ; we would have to show the relationship between Ghiberti and his predecessors—e.g., Giovanni Pisano and the Master Bonanus—and between him and his contemporaries, e.g., Lorenzo Monaco, Masaccio, Donatello, Jacopo della Quercia, Pisanello, Sluter and Van Eyck. Ghiberti is, after all, only partly a Renaissance artist and, to take a single point, we ought to indicate the difference

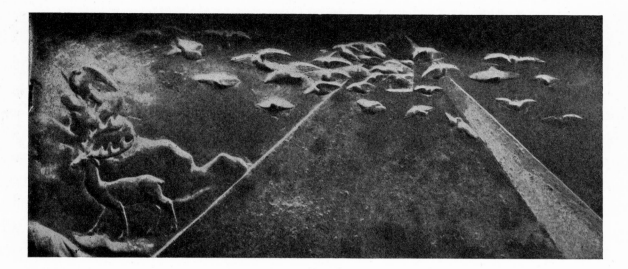

Fig. 3. Two details from Ghiberti's Noah relief (plate 52)

between his employment of perspective and perspective as it is used by the first generation of Renaissance artists; or, again, at least in general terms, his indebtedness to Northern goldsmith work. But all that would form the subject-matter of a comprehensive history of Italian Quattrocento sculpture rather than of a short essay. Here we can only mention that the longing to reproduce nature by means of sculpture found expression in Italian poetry at a time when art itself was still content with the old forms. In the Purgatorio (Canto X) Dante describes some carvings and praises their faithfulness to nature : " Reliefs which would put to shame not only Polycletus but nature herself."

This desire for illusion in sculpture was not satisfied until a hundred years after Dante. Ghiberti's remarkable technique of freeing the foreground figures, of making the backgrounds recede, his free use of light and shade—all these things which have so often been blamed as false, serve merely to create the effect of illusion.

The great problem in art in Ghiberti's time was how to render spatial depth. The artists discovered perspective (that is to say, the relativity of all lines) and shading (that is to say, the relativity of all forms which are dependent on light and on their distance from the eye). It was not until the nineteenth century that the Impressionists applied the same scientific spirit to art.

III

" The essence of all art is the representation of ideas, and ideas are substantially visual."

Schopenhauer, 1837

THIS change in the method of artistic representation, from the essential and absolute to the apparent and subjective, was accompanied, in the world of about 1400, by a change of subject-matter. Preference was now given to the individual, as is shown by the rise of portraiture, and there was a leaning towards genre-like subjects, towards homely, rational, literary or decorative themes, together with a corresponding turning away from the ecstatic and the heroic. In everyday life this victory of reason coincided with the development of new political conditions and a new evaluation of those forces to which the control of the mind is reserved. The humanists supplanted the clergy, the merchants the knights, the guilds the Senate, and knowledge took the place of faith. Florence—for all this applies more to Florence than to the other cities lying between Naples and Bruges—became a democratic state, ruled by bankers and industrialists. Revolts against this new order—such as that of the *Ciompi* or wool-beaters in the year of Ghiberti's birth—occurred without producing any lasting effect and victory remained with the middle classes, above all with the big merchants, embodied in their guilds. Ghiberti's patrons were not clerics or princes, but mercantile associations.

What they appreciated, what they wanted and paid for, was homely, that is to say realistic art. It would be wrong to maintain that this change of political conditions brought about the change in the tendency of art, but one can at least say that the new spirit, which found its readiest expression in art, carried everyday life along with it, shaped politics and helped realism to achieve victory in every field. In other Italian city states the process was slower; in Bologna, for example, Quercia had still to deal with patrons who belonged to a highly cultured clergy, whereas Ghiberti's bronze doors in Florence were ordered by shopkeepers who knew what they liked, but had no knowledge of theology, and who engaged a humanist, instead of a theologian, to draw up the programme for the second door. Only the Medici, who were also among Ghiberti's patrons, were everything rolled into one—traders, patrons of art and scholars. But they too had no interest in religious works of art such as were commissioned by the Church in the days of St Francis; the religious pictures which they ordered and paid for were worldly enough—the Madonna became a pretty Florentine girl, the angels were all too like the street-urchins or apprentices who posed as models for them, the surrounding saints were portraits of well-known Florentine merchants and their relatives. We must consider Ghiberti's Old Testament reliefs, not as religious legends, but as *novelle*. (Florentine literature underwent a similar transformation from Jacopo da Todi and Dante to Boccaccio.) The city of Florence had never shown any particular enthusiasm for religion and had never indulged in processions of flagellants or taken part in crusades; and it was left to Cosimo de' Medici to say : " God was never to be found in my books as a debtor."

Ghiberti was given religious subjects by his patrons, but the manner in which he executed them won for him the esteem of the guilds and of Cosimo.

IV

In the early days of the Renaissance a Florentine would walk into an artist's workshop with as little hesitation as when we today enter any shop, and would there give his orders—for anything from a decorated button to a painted altar-piece or a marble tomb could be ordered in the same workshop. The carpenter, the interior-decorator, the book-illustrator, the goldsmith—in those days these were not yet specialized professions, although certain artists, according to their talents, might eventually show a preference for one special branch of art. Even Leonardo and Michelangelo did not consider themselves above any kind of work, whether it were a trinket, a sword hilt, the scenery for a theatre, the layout of a garden or even the erection of a snowman, and every great Florentine painter was prepared to paint bedsteads and clothes-chests.

The profession of artist was at that time like any other profession. The artist was an artisan, and as such, was obliged to join a guild. Brunelleschi was once arrested while at work, because he was not enrolled in the right guild. (The development of associations of artists starts from the masons' yards, the organization of which had much in common with that of the monastic and chivalrous orders, and leads to the guilds, which were associations of merchants and artisans, and finally to the academies, in which gifted artists assembled to form an elect and authoritative parliament of the intellect.)

In 1409 Ghiberti joined the guild of the goldsmiths, in 1423 that of the painters, and in 1427 that of the stonemasons. His master in the goldsmith's art was Bartoluccio di Michele.

In 1443 the Florentine authorities received an anonymous denunciation alleging that Ghiberti was not the son of Cione da Pelago, " a worthless and almost forgotten man ", but the illegitimate child of Bartoluccio and Monna Fiore ; the latter was, it was true, married to Cione, but was living in adultery with Bartoluccio, to whom, it was alleged, she bore a son, Lorenzo Ghiberti, in 1378, and whom she married in 1406, after the death of Cione.

This denunciation was rejected as being a calumny, but it is impossible to affirm with certainty that it was unfounded. In any case, Bartoluccio appears to have brought Ghiberti up and adopted him ; he also taught him the goldsmith's art and had him instructed in that of painting, though we do not know in what atelier. If Baldinucci is to be believed, Ghiberti's teacher was Gherardo Starnina. His first independent works were paintings.

In 1400 plague once more broke out in Florence and between 1st May and 18th September 10,908 people died of it. Ghiberti, in company of another young painter, fled to Pesaro, but his step-father remained in Florence. Writing in 1400, a Florentine notary, Ser Lapo Mazzei, describes the desolation of Florence : " Hardly a shop is ever opened. The merchants do not come to their offices. The Palaggio Maggiore is without officials ; you find no one in the assembly hall. They weep no more for the dead and people free from fear are to be seen only on biers."

In Pesaro Ghiberti painted a wall in the castle of the Malatestas. Shortly afterwards he heard that there was to be a competition for the second door of the Baptistery and returned to Florence in order to take part in it. Bartoluccio helped him
with his designs and he won the competition against Brunelleschi, Jacopo della
Quercia and four other artists.

In November 1403 the contract for the second door—which was Ghiberti's
first—was signed and this was the beginning of his fifty years' activity as a sculptor.

There is no need for me to give here a detailed list of his works, for that was
done by Ghiberti himself in his account of his life (which is given in translation in
the following pages). The historical and documentary details which I can add to
this account will be found in the Notes on the Plates. To avoid repetition, I will
therefore limit myself to mentioning a few lost works and some details on his
journeys and his career.

In 1416 Ghiberti married Marsilia, who was then fifteen years old ; their first son,
Tommaso, was born in 1417, and their second, Vettorio, who later became Ghiberti's
most valuable collaborator on the " Gate of Paradise ", two years later.

From 1401 to 1417 Ghiberti appears to have remained in Florence, but in the
latter year he went with two journeymen, Guglielmo and Bartolomeo, to Siena,
his expenses for this journey being paid by the Cathedral authorities, including even
such items as money spent on bread and oranges, for the hire of a packhorse, and for
the sojourn of the master and his two assistants at the " Cock " tavern. Ghiberti
brought back with him from Siena a commission for two bronze reliefs.

In April 1424 the plague broke out again and Ghiberti, with all his assistants,
fled to Venice. A year later the reliefs for the font in Siena had not been completed
and the only letters of Ghiberti's which have been preserved date from this period.
The most interesting of these is one addressed to Giovanni Turini, goldsmith in
Siena, which reads as follows :—

" My worthy friend,

I received your letter of the fourteenth of April, from which I see that you
are my true and devoted friend and furthermore that you are well . . . and that
you still bear me that good will which you have ever borne me, in that you
would, if it were necessary, aid me in the chasing and polishing of one of these
histories, and that you would, as you say, do it with pleasure. This, I know, can
but spring from your great love for me, for which God bless you. Know then,
dear friend, that the histories are well nigh finished—one is in the hands of
Giuliano di Ser Andrea and one I have with me, and they will be finished at the
time which I promised to Messer Bartolomeo. Indeed they would long since
have been finished, had it not been for the ingratitude of those who in the past
assisted me and from whom I have received not one, but many injuries. By
God's grace I am now rid of them, for which I shall ever praise Him, mindful
of the freedom I now enjoy. Alone, without assistants, I will remain, for I would
fain be master of my own workshop and receive each one of my friends with a
serene and joyful countenance. I thank you for the great good will you bear me
and beg you to recommend me warmly to Messer Bartolomeo. Also I entreat
you urgently that you contrive in some wise that I may receive again the

drawings of birds which I lent to Ghoro [di Ser Neroccio, goldsmith of Siena]. I know that you can without difficulty ask Master Domenicho [di Niccolò] the wood-carver to send them to me, for I have learned that they and all other things that were in the hands of Ghoro, are now in those of Master Domenicho. Greet him from me, and likewise Master Francesco di Valdambrino. And if for my part there is aught I can do here, I am always at your pleasure. There is naught else to say. May Jesus Christ keep you in peace.

This sixteenth day of April 1425.

From your dear friend Lorenzo di Bartolo,

goldsmith of Florence."*

Towards the end of his life, probably in 1447, Ghiberti was in Rome. We do not know whether, during his stay there, following the example of Brunelleschi and Donatello, he merely studied and admired antique art, or whether he actually executed works in Rome (as Gelli, writing in about 1550, suggested). Of works by Ghiberti's hand in Rome at that time there were two papal mitres and a morse for a cope, but these, too, like all his other goldsmith's work, have long since been lost, and the same fate has befallen the two candlesticks for Or San Michele, which Guariento made after designs by Ghiberti in 1417.

That nothing of Ghiberti's goldsmith's work has come down to us would appear to be a great loss, in view of the high praise which Cellini bestowed upon him in his treatise on this branch of art (1568) :

"Lorenzo Ghiberti ! He was a goldsmith indeed ! Not only in the wonderfulness of his own peculiar style, but because of his unwearied power of marvellous finish and his exceeding diligence in execution. This man, who must be counted among the most admirable of goldsmiths, applied himself to everything, but especially to the shaping of smaller works. And though now and then he set about doing larger pieces, he did his best in the production of small figures, and in this branch we may well call him a master of the art of chasing. Indeed, he pursued this with such excellence that, as is still obvious to all, no man can rival him ! "

Albertini recommended that bronzes should be cast in a thickness not greater than that of a knife's edge, in order to avoid their being used one day for the casting of cannon. In wartime nothing could save heavy gold ornaments such as Ghiberti produced from being melted down. Our only consolation is the fact that all his other works, with one or two exceptions, are still in their original locations. For five hundred years they have stood in the places where Ghiberti erected them.

---

*Ghiberti's friend, Giovanni Turini, made two of the reliefs for the same font ; Goro di Neroccio, mentioned in the letter, contributed the figure of Fortitude, but at the time when the letter was written, he was already dead. The drawings of birds which Ghiberti lent to him—one is involuntarily reminded of the birds on the framework of the "Gate of Paradise"—passed after his death into the possession of the wood-carver, Domenico di Niccolò, and Ghiberti was thus asking for the restitution of his own property. It is not surprising that so many reliefs and statuettes have been attributed to Ghiberti, if he allowed his drawings to be used even outside his workshop. Francesco di Valdambrino, to whom he sends such friendly greetings, was one of his rivals in the competition of 1401.

V

" We, the artists of ancient times, shall live for ever : not in the schools of word-mongers, but in the circle of the wise, where they do not talk of Andromache's mother and Niobe's sons, but of the deep causes of things human and divine."

Pico della Mirandola, 1485

GHIBERTI was a very slow worker. It took him years to produce a piece of jewellery or a slab for a tomb, or even a reliquary. He spent three years on each of the large figures for Or San Michele and about the same time on chasing a single bronze relief after it had been cast. He started on his two bronze doors when he was a very young man, and more than fifty years later, after his death (he died on 1st December 1455 and was buried in Santa Croce) his son went on working for years on the frame. And with all that, Ghiberti employed many assistants, sometimes as many as twenty, promising young artists like Donatello, Paolo Uccello, Gozzoli, perhaps also Pollaiulo and Luca della Robbia, among them. The years passed and still his work was not finished, but his patrons did not lose patience with him. "I shall be expelled," said Cosimo de' Medici, "but my buildings will remain."

Technical skill has made great strides since those days. We could probably cast the whole of Ghiberti's door in one piece. But in his time the first casting of a bronze was often a failure—this happened with one of Ghiberti's figures for Or San Michele and also with the frame of one of his doors. The same thing happened with works of Donatello and with Michelangelo's statue of Julius in Bologna. We, today, know how to do these things, but yet we cannot do them.

Those who are surprised and grieved that we cannot produce such beautiful works as the artists of the Renaissance, do not realize what labour it cost at that time. Twenty years passed before Verrocchio's "St Thomas" was finished; Leonardo da Vinci spent thirty years considering the equestrian monument of Sforza; after forty years, Michelangelo had contrived to hew out of the marble one Moses and two slaves for his monument to Julius; and it took another man his whole life to produce two doors. We have not the same patience, nor the same faith in the value of beautiful things; we cannot wait so long for a single work. We know how short life is and we do not quite believe that art is long. Thus our works spring up as quickly as weeds.

But in Florence, while all Italy was waging war—city against city, faction against faction, clan against clan, caste against caste—while Turks and Frenchmen and Spaniards were threatening the country with slaughter and rape, whilst the plague returned to ravage the city time after time, the people were listening to their most spiritual preachers, they were reading the books of their saints and of their classical scholars, spelling out the texts of Plato and Homer, and decorating their houses and churches, painting their pictures and carving their statues, knowing that these works would outlive the storms and conflagrations of incessant war.

GHIBERTI'S AUTOBIOGRAPHY[(1)]

WRITTEN ABOUT 1445[(2)]

[¶1] I, O most honoured patron, did not join in the chase after lucre, but occupied myself solely with Art, to which I had eagerly and whole-heartedly dedicated myself from childhood. For I have ever striven to observe her fundamental laws, to examine the ways of nature, to discover how pictures are conceived, how the sense of sight works and in what manner the canons of painting and sculpture can be determined.
[¶2] When I was young, not only the plague, but also the evil conditions reigning in my native city[3] caused me to leave Florence in the year of Our Lord 1400, in the company of a gifted painter[4] in the employ of our noble Duke Malatesta of Pesaro,[5] who requested us to execute murals in one of his rooms.[6] A commission which we carried out with zest. At that time it was my intention to devote myself solely to the art of Painting, a decision in which I was fortified by my companion, who convinced me of the honour and credit we should derive from such works as our benefactor was proposing to offer us. My friends in the meantime wrote to me that the wardens of the Church of San Giovanni were seeking masters of proven ability, requesting them to submit examples of their work. In order to comply with this request and participate in the competition, a host of accomplished masters journeyed thither from all parts of Italy.
[¶3] Whereupon I, too, begged permission to take farewell of our Duke and of my companion; when the former heard of this matter he imme-diately granted my request; and so I joined the other artists offering their services to the Masters of the Works of the aforementioned Church. Each of us was furnished with four sheets of bronze. The wardens and officials at the head of the undertaking demanded that each artist give proof of his powers by conceiving a design for a plaque of a specified door, the identical subject—The Sacrifice of Isaac—to be treated by all the competitors. A year was allowed for the trial work and whoever was acclaimed the winner should be entrusted with the entire work. The competitors comprised the following: Filippo, son of Ser Brunellesco,[7] Simone da Colle, Niccolò d'Arezzo, Jacopo della Quercia from Siena, Francesco di Valdambrino,[7A] Niccolò Lamberti. We were six [not counting myself] who were permitted to enter the com-petition. This trial demanded a considerable knowledge of the sculp-tor's art. Without a single dissenting voice the experts as well as my fellow competitors honoured me by the presentation of the victor's palm. All without exception were at this time of the opinion that I had, whilst submitting to the supervision of learned judges, surpassed the other competitors by my efforts.[8]
[¶4] The aforementioned Masters of the Works of San Giovanni pre-sented me with a special testimonial of their own; they were men of great experience, not only in the art of painting, but expert also in the fashioning of gold, silver and marble. Thirty-four judges, drawn in part from the city, in part from surrounding places, all agreed in testifying to my victory. These comprised the Consuls and Priors, as well as the entire Corporation of the Cloth Merchants' Guild, who

Fig. 4. Francesco di Valdambrino: Angel of the Annunciation. Wood, painted and gilded. About 1410. Montepulciano, Duomo

controlled all matters relating to the Church of San Giovanni. Thus it was that I received the commission to make the bronze door of the said Church; and this, my first important work, was executed with particular diligence.[9] The cost thereof, including the decorated frame surround-ing the two wings of the door, amounted to about twenty-two thousand florins.[10]
[¶5] The door in question is divided into twenty-eight panels, twenty of which disclose the stories of the New Testament, and in the lower rows four Evangelists and four Doctors of the Church, all surrounded by a large number of heads. The whole work, including the borders of ivy, is executed with much care and industry, as also the modelling of the jambs, which are conceived as a rich frame decorated with varie-gated foliage. The total weight of the work ran into thirty-four thousand pounds. It truly was carried out with considerable under-standing and artifice.
[¶6] At this same time I was commissioned to execute a statue of St John the Baptist,[11] measuring four and a third cubits[12]; it was cast in fine bronze and erected in the year 1414.
[¶7] The Municipality of Siena ordered me to design a work illustrating two stories, that of St John baptizing Christ, and a second in which he is led captive before Herod; both of these were placed in the Baptistery there.[13]

---

[1] The Autobiography forms a part of the second book of Ghiberti's *Commentarii*. The original manuscript has been lost, but there is a copy by an almost contemporary hand in the Biblioteca Nazionale at Florence; this copy was used by Vasari and in his time belonged to his learned friend Cosimo Bartoli; it was transcribed and edited by Julius von Schlosser (*I Commentarii*, Berlin, 1912, 2 vols.). The first *commentario* contains an epitome of antique art history, after Athenaeus, Vitruvius and Pliny; the second part deals with Trecento painters and sculptors since Giotto; the third with the theoretical principles of the visual arts, and contains also descriptions of antique sculptures which Ghiberti saw in Rome, Padua and Siena.

[2] Ghiberti must have written his Autobiography not later than 1445, or perhaps in the first months of 1446, because Filippo Brunelleschi is mentioned as alive—he died on April 15, 1446—and Ghiberti says he intends to write in collaboration with him a treatise on architecture. On the other hand, the Autobiography contains remarks on the small statues and heads on the frame of the second door, which decorations do not seem to have been cast until 1448, if we understand the documents correctly. One may assume that Ghiberti, while proceeding with the framework of his master-piece, made some additions to the text, without taking care to bring certain points up to date.

[3] Florence was at war with Gian Galeazzo Visconti, Duke of Milan, and Florentine émigrés (including members of the Medici, Alberti, Strozzi and Altoviti families) plotted against the city. Machiavelli tells the story at length. In 1400 Ghiberti was 22.

[4] Gelli, about 1550, called this painter *Piserino*. Perkins (p. 8) thinks that this companion was Antonio Vite, who worked in Pisa. The only Florentine painter who seems to have worked at that time in Pesaro is Mariotto di Nardo; in the Museum of Pesaro there is a triptych by his hand, a Madonna with St Francis and St Michael, dated 1400.

[5] Pandolfo Malatesta il Senatore, 1386-1429. Vasari, Baldinucci, Perkins and others, maintain that Ghiberti worked also for the Malatesta in Rimini; this mistake is apparently due merely to the fact that the Malatesta of Rimini are better known than the Malatesta of Pesaro.

[6] Baldinucci believed that Ghiberti's painting master was Gherardo Starnina.

[7] Plate 2. [7A] Compare fig. 4. [8] Plate 3.

[9] Plate 5.

[10] The purchasing value of the florin was very great: one paid, for instance, one florin for about 150 lb. of wheat towards the end of the 15th century in Florence. According to Muentz, a burgher in Florence of the same period needed at least fifty florins a year; but fashionable living cost two hundred or more. Pope Martin V agreed in 1427 to a yearly payment of three hundred florins to Gentile da Fabriano; the sculptor Bernardo Rossellino received fifteen florins a month.

[11] Plate 100. [12] The Florentine cubit equals c. 23 inches. [13] Plates 107 and 108.

¶[8] Furthermore, I completed with my own hands a bronze statue of St Matthew four and a half cubits high.[14]

¶[9] I also made a bronze memorial slab for Leonardo Dati, general of the Dominicans.[15] He was an exceedingly learned man and I modelled him from life. The plaque is in bas-relief with an inscription at the feet of its recumbent figure.

¶[10] I also supervised the execution, in marble, of memorial tablets to Lodovico degli Obizzi and to Bartolommeo Valori, who lie buried in the cemetery of the Minorite friars.[16]

¶[11] Furthermore, in Santa Maria degli Angeli, the home of the Benedictine monks, is a bronze casket by me, containing bones of the three martyrs, Protus, Hyacinth and Nemesius. On the front of the casket two angels in relief bear an olive wreath in their hands, which encloses an inscription of their holy names.[17]

¶[12] At this same time I set in gold a cornelian about the size of a walnut inclusive of its shell; on its surface are engraved three figures

Figs. 5-6.   Apollo and Marsyas. Copies of an antique cornelian ; a bronze plaquette (in Berlin Museum) and an engraving from "Gemmæ Antiquæ, per Leonardum Augustinum ad Celsitudinem Cosmi Principis Etruriæ", vol. II, 1669

from the hand of an excellent old Master. I conceived a dragon to serve as clasp for the jewel; the head drooped from the neck being bent in the middle, and its wings, slightly outspread, served as a handle to the whole.   The dragon, or rather, let us say, the winged serpent, was surrounded by ivy leaves, and around the aforesaid figures with my own hand I engraved the name—Nero—in antique lettering.[18] I took great pains with this work.[19] The figures on the cornelian consisted of an old man sitting upon a rock covered by a lion's skin, his hands being tied behind his back to a tree stump. A lad kneeling upon one leg looks up at a youth bearing a scroll in his right and a lyre in his left hand; apparently the lad is seeking instruction from the youth. Obviously the intention was to depict the three ages of man. I am convinced that the piece emanated from the hand of Pyrgoteles or Polycletus. I have never seen a more perfect example of a gem engraved in intaglio.

¶[13] When Pope Martin came to Florence he gave me orders for a golden mitre[20] and a pectoral clasp for a pluvial;[21] upon the former I made eight demi-figures in gold, and upon the clasp the figure of Our Lord in the act of blessing.

---

[14] Plate 102.   [15] Plate 124.   [16] Plates 122 and 123.   [17] Plate 111.

[18] On the fashion of the *litteræ antiquæ*, especially favoured by Niccolò Niccoli and Poggio, see Voigt, *Die Wiederbelebung des classischen Alterthums*, vol. I, 3rd ed., 1893, p. 398.

[19] *Apollo and Marsyas; see* note 12 on page 24; mentioned in the Medici Inventory of 1492 and valued at 1000 florins. The date of Ghiberti's work should be about 1428. The gem is now lost, and we know nothing about the setting, whereas the cornelian is preserved in many imitations (cf. figs. 5-6). Florentine painting, too, has preserved illustrations of this famous *intaglio*: It is depicted as a medallion round the neck of the so-called beautiful Simonetta (School of Botticelli, Frankfurt, Staedel Institute) and also in the left lower corner of the *Didimus* title page of 1488, painted by the miniaturist Gherardo di Giovanni for Matthias Corvin and now in the Morgan Library in New York. (Molinier, *Les Plaquettes*, I, 1886, p. 4f.; Carl Frey, *Michelagniolo*, *Quellen und Forschungen*, I, 1907, p. 92f.; also in his edition of the *Codice Magliabechiano*, 1892, pp. 275-278; Eric Maclagan, *Catalogue of Italian Plaquettes in the Victoria and Albert Museum*, 1924, p. 13f.)

[20] Pope Martin V was in Florence in 1419. His golden mitre, and the other one, made for Pope Eugenius IV and mentioned below, are now lost. It seems that they were still extant early in the 16th century, if we may judge from the following two passages. In 1511 Stazio Gaddio, the tutor of Federigo Gonzaga, writes in a letter: "*The Pope [Julius II] is very fond of trinkets. Yesterday he ordered that his two tiaras should be brought in. The one is worth two hundred thousand ducats, the other one hundred thousand. I believe never in my life shall I see again things of such beauty and so richly decorated with pearls and jewels.*" The other reference is from Benvenuto Cellini's Autobiography and relates an incident of 1527: "*While the Pope [Clement VII] was besieged [by the Constable Charles de Bourbon] in Castel Sant' Angelo, the jewels were taken from their settings and the tiaras molten down.*" One of these tiaras was probably by Ghiberti.

[21] A pluvial is (according to Samuel Johnson) a priest's cope. The shape of the cope explains the use of this word—in mediæval Latin *pluvial* meant a rain-coat. In later times the word designated the coronation robe of the Emperors and the cloak of the Popes.

Fig. 7.   God the Father Blessing. Florentine xv century engraving, perhaps based on Ghiberti's morse for Pope Martin V. Florence, Uffizi

¶[14] And when Pope Eugenius likewise made his abode in the city of Florence[22] he, too, called me in to execute a golden mitre whose weight in metal amounted to fifteen pounds; the jewels alone weighed five and a half pounds. They were valued at 38,000 florins by the jewellers of our city, and were composed of balas rubies, sapphires, emeralds and pearls. The aforesaid mitre contained six pearls, each the size of a hazelnut. It was decorated besides with many figures and rich ornament. On the front face Our Lord on a throne surrounded by a multitude of angels,[23] on the reverse Our Lady likewise enthroned with angelic beings about her, in the golden quatrefoils[24] the four Evangelists, and on the frieze at the base a multitude of cherubs; the whole work being carried out with great splendour.

¶[15] After this I received a commission from the Wool Merchants' Guild to execute a bronze statue four and a half cubits high, which they erected outside the oratory of Or San Michele.[25] It represented Saint Stephen and was made—according to my custom—with great care.

¶[16] The Master of the Works of the Cathedral also ordered of me a bronze casket for the remains of Saint Zenobius, three and a half cubits long.[26] This was decorated in relief with scenes from the life of the Saint. He is depicted on the front resuscitating a child left in his care by its mother till the latter should have returned from a pilgrimage.[27] Furthermore, how the child died whilst the woman was on her travels, and how on her return the Saint, being asked for the child now dead, revived it; and how another child is killed by a cart.[28] Also visible is the scene in which one of two messengers (sent to him by St Ambrose) having been killed in the Alps, is brought back to him.[29] His companion is shown mourning over the dead man, while St Zenobius says, *Go, why do you sleep? you will find him alive*, and he continued his journey and really did find him living. On the reverse six angels hold a wreath of elm leaves encircling an inscription in antique lettering commemorating the Saint.[30]

¶[17] At long last I was commissioned to produce the other i.e. the third[31] door of the Baptistery and received a free hand to carry out this work as I thought fit, which meant that it would be conceived perfectly

---

[22] Pope Eugenius IV came to Florence the first time in 1434; in 1436 he consecrated the Cathedral of Florence, and in 1439 the crypt for Ghiberti's chest of St Zanobi.

[23] According to Ghiberti's own description, the clasp of Martin V showed Our Lord blessing, the front of Eugenius IV's mitre Our Lord enthroned and surrounded by Angels. A small engraving by an unknown Florentine goldsmith of the 15th century may have been made either from the one or the other design (fig. 7), as it answers quite well to the description and its style can be connected with the Ghiberti *sportello* (pl. 118). All goldsmith's work by Ghiberti has been lost.

[24] That means, each figure was in a Gothic frame in the shape of four-leaved clover. The plaques of the first door are framed in the same way (pl. 5).

[25] Plate 104.   [26] Plate 112-C.   [27] Plate 113.   [28] Plate 112-A.   [29] Plate 112-B.

[30] Plate 112.   [31] Plate 45.

and executed with splendour and a wealth of ornament. So I began working out the panels measuring one and a third cubits which were to illustrate, with a multitude of figures, stories from the Old Testament. I took great pains to observe all the rules of proportion and, as far as lay in my power, to imitate nature in just relationships and contours. In some stories I introduced nigh a hundred figures, in some less, and in others more. Truly I worked with the greatest diligence and love. There were ten stories altogether and all the architectural settings introduced were in perspective, and so true to life that they looked like sculpture in the round seen from the right distance. They are carried out in very low relief and the figures visible on the nearer planes are bigger than those on the distant ones, just as they appear in real life. The whole work was executed with these proportions kept well in mind. As I mentioned before, there were ten stories. The first[32] shows the creation of Man and Woman, and how they disobey the Creator of all Things; in the same scene you see them driven out of Paradise on account of the sin they committed; thus in one and the same panel no less than four acts are portrayed. In the second[33] panel Adam and Eve have become the parents of Cain and Abel, who appear here as little children. Then there are seen offering sacrifices to the Lord, Cain, the smaller and poorer one, while Abel gives the handsomest and the best—the latter's offering being most pleasing to God, whilst that of Cain is quite the reverse. Following upon this you observe Cain killing Abel out of jealousy. In this panel Abel minds the flocks, while Cain tills the soil. The next scene represents God appearing to Cain and asking him about the brother whom he has killed. In this panel, as also in the four that follow, four scenes are depicted in each one. In the third[34] you behold Noah, his wife, sons and daughters-in-law, the animals and birds, all emerging from the Ark and then how he and his tribe are offering sacrifices. Furthermore, the planting of the vine, Noah's subsequent drunkenness, the mocking of his son, Ham, and the covering of his nakedness by his two other sons. In the fourth panel,[35] the three Angels appear to Abraham, who prays to one of them, while his servants and ass remain at the foot of the mountain, also the scene in which he has unrobed Isaac and is about to sacrifice him but for the Angel, who, pointing at the ram, stays the hand that holds the knife. In the fifth panel,[36] Esau and Jacob are born, the former is sent out hunting and their Mother, led by Jacob, brings him the kid, whose skin she lays over his shoulders while she tells him to beg Isaac's blessing—and Isaac, feeling his back and finding it hairy, blesses him. In the sixth,[37] how Joseph is thrown into the well by his brothers, is sold into bondage and brought before Pharaoh, King of Egypt. How he interprets Pharaoh's dream as a prophecy of a great famine, which is due to break out in Egypt, whereby he conceives means for combating it, so that all districts and regions receive grants of food according to their need and are saved; in consequence of which Joseph is held in great honour by Pharaoh. Then there is the scene in which Jacob sends his sons and Joseph, recognizing his brothers[38], informs them that unless they return with their brother, Benjamin, they will not receive any grain. They come back with Benjamin, for whom Joseph prepares a meal, ordering a cup to be placed in his pack, which being found Benjamin is brought before Joseph, who makes himself known to his brothers.[39] In the seventh panel[40] Moses receives the Tablets of the Law upon the mountain top, whilst Joshua remains halfway up, and the multitude is terrified by the raging of lightning, thunder and earthquake, and stands astonished at the foot of the mountain. In the eighth,[41] how Joshua sets out against Jericho, arrives at the river Jordan and erects twelve tents. How he surrounds the city, gives orders for trumpets to be blown, and how, after seven days, the walls totter and the city is captured. In the ninth panel[42] David kills Goliath and the people of Israel defeat the Philistines. Then David, returning with the head of Goliath,[43] is greeted by the people dancing and declaiming the words *Saul killed his thousands, but David his tens of thousands.* In the tenth,[44] the Queen of Sheba and a great retinue arrive to visit Solomon; she is richly clad and around her congregates a great crowd.

¶18] The friezes framing the stories contain twenty-four figures, and the same number of heads appear between one frieze and another.[45] This is the most outstanding of my works and I laboured at it with the utmost ardour and technical attainment, completing it with all possible artistry, sense of proportion and knowledge of art. In the outermost borders on the door case and cornice a decorative pattern of foliage, birds and all sorts of small creatures[46] are introduced in a manner fitting for such type of ornamentation. In addition, the inside of the door-case is adorned with bas-relief decoration in bronze shaped with greatest art, and even the threshold is likewise ornamented.

¶19] However, in order not to tire readers, I shall refrain from mentioning other works produced by me. I know that such things will be of no particular interest; therefore, I beg my readers to show forbearance and

Fig. 8. The Dome of Florence Cathedral

exercise patience. For I also assisted many painters, sculptors and masons to attain honour with their works by furnishing them with models in wax and clay. Painters in particular received sketch designs in quantities, those who had to execute figures over life size were given rules and the correct method for making them.[47]

¶20] On the front of Santa Maria del Fiore I designed an Assumption of the Madonna[48] for the central circular window, likewise those on either side. Many another design for stained glass in the abovementioned church is mine. Three circular windows in the choir are from my hand. The first displays Christ ascending unto heaven,[49] the second His prayer on the Mount of Olives,[50] and the third His presentation in the Temple.[51] Few things of importance in our region were produced that were not designed and arranged by my hand.

¶21] Both receiving an identical wage, Filippo Brunelleschi[52] and I laboured side by side on the cupola of the Cathedral for eighteen years and in this time brought the work to a successful conclusion. We also propose to write a treatise on architecture in which we shall elaborate this theme.

[47] This opens a wide field for speculation, particularly as Uccello and Gozzoli belonged to Ghiberti's workshop, and perhaps also Filarete, Luca della Robbia, Bernardo Rossellino and Antonio Pollaiuolo. Giving full rein to one's imagination, one might suspect that Ghiberti designed in 1436 the Hawkwood memorial for Uccello, or that some of the reliefs on Pollaiuolo's silver cross were made from the master's designs; or could he have helped Gozzoli with the two Madonnas in Montefalco? All this would be wild guess work, perhaps more amusing but even worse grounded than the futile attempts to attribute vast numbers of terracottas to Ghiberti.

[48] Plate 129. [49] Plate 132. [50] Plate 131. [51] Plate 130.

[52] See Fabriczy, *Filippo Brunelleschi*, 1892, pp. 108-118.—Here is an epitome of the dates concerning Ghiberti's activities as an architect:

1404, Nov. 10. Ghiberti appears, together with Brunelleschi, before the Commission for the consideration of the work on the superstructure of the nave of the Cathedral.

1406, Feb. 16. This Commission is broken up and Ghiberti and Brunelleschi are dismissed from office as advisers to the *Opera*.

1418. Ghiberti submits two models for the cupola of the Cathedral.

1420, April. Brunelleschi's model accepted. He, together with Ghiberti, and Battista d'Antonio, head of the works, appointed as *provveditori* (supervisors, master-builders) for the building of the cupola at the salary of 3 florins each.

1425, Feb. 5. Ghiberti and Brunelleschi re-elected as *provveditori*.

1425, June 28. Ghiberti's salary temporarily suspended.

1426, Febr. 4. Ghiberti relieved of his duties.

1429, Sept. 22. Ghiberti and Brunelleschi commissioned to make a model of the whole Cathedral.

1432, Mar. 10. Competition for the tomb of St Zenobius in Florence Cathedral won by Ghiberti.

1433, Jan. 31. Ghiberti finally abandons the supervision of the building of the Cathedral.

1435. Ghiberti takes part in the competition for the designing of the new choir of the Cathedral—won by Brunelleschi.

1436. Ghiberti competes in the designing of the lantern of the cupola—Brunelleschi's model approved.

[32] Plate 46. [33] Plate 51. [34] Plate 52. [35] Plate 55. [36] Plate 57. [37] Plate 61.
[38] Plate 63. [39] Plate 62. [40] Plate 65. [41] Plate 67. [42] Plate 69. [43] Plate 70.
[44] Plate 71. [45] Plates 73-98. [46] E.g. plates 74-76.

LIFE OF LORENZO GHIBERTI
PAINTER[1] OF FLORENCE
BY GIORGIO VASARI · 1568

Fig. 9. Ghiberti and Brunelleschi offering the model of a church to Cosimo de' Medici. Fresco in the Palazzo Vecchio, Florence, by Giorgio Vasari

[¶1] LORENZO was the son of Bartoluccio Ghiberti,[2] and learned the art of a goldsmith with his father from his earliest years, for the latter was an excellent workman, and taught his son that trade, so that he was soon surpassed by his pupil. But Lorenzo took far more pleasure in the art of sculpture and of design, sometimes using colours, and at other times making small figures of bronze, finishing them with much grace. He was also very fond of imitating the dies of antique coins and medals, and made the portraits of many of his friends.[3]

[¶2] Whilst he was working with Bartoluccio and endeavouring to become proficient in that profession, the plague broke out in Florence in the year 1400, as he himself relates in a book he has written upon matters relating to the arts, which is in the possession of the venerable M. Cosimo Bartoli, a nobleman of Florence. In addition to the plague, many civil discords and other troubles were rife in the city, obliging him to leave it, and he set out in company with another painter to the

the other, Lorenzo could not be admitted to the offices of the City. The Conservadori wished to discover the truth of the matter for the sake both of their own honour and of that of the community, and had Lorenzo charged with transgression of the law. He was summoned forthwith to plead his cause and proved most conclusively by official documents of 1374 that Fiore had been the lawful wife of Cione and that he himself had been born in 1378 in the said lawful wedlock; and that later, after the death of his father Cione, Fiore had in second marriage taken Bartoluccio, who had adopted him, Lorenzo, when he was quite young, had reared him, having no other sons, and had taught him his craft of a goldsmith. Thus it had come about that Bartoluccio had been regarded as Lorenzo's father by everybody; wherefore the people had always called him Lorenzo di Bartoluccio. To confirm these statements he showed that after Cione's death he, as the son, had in 1413 recovered from his relatives certain goods which the said Cione, his father, had lent to Maso degli Albizzi, a citizen in high esteem at the time. He also said that he had paid the taxes from 1422 onwards, though under the name of Bartoluccio. But as the law laid down that whoever had not paid the communal taxes for thirty years was unable to hold any of the offices of the City, Lorenzo was on his own evidence fined by the Conservadori di Legge five hundred lire as a trespasser. As regards the other charge of illegitimacy, he was acquitted; the accusation or denunciation was declared slanderous and he was confirmed to be the legitimate son of Cione di Ser Buonaccorso of Pelago. Some time after this sentence Lorenzo appealed to the Signoria, namely to the Gonfaloniere and the Priori, the Gonfalonieri di Compagnia and the Dodici Buonuomini, declaring that after such condemnation by the Conservadori di Legge he had found that his father Cione had since the year 1375 been exempted from the taxes of Florentine citizens; and he made a petition that he himself should therefore be absolved and released of the said fine of five hundred lire. The Signoria, acknowledging these things, absolved him thereof and re-affirmed that he was the son of Cione di Ser Buonaccorso, but was commonly known as Lorenzo di Bartoluccio; and if he happened to be elected to such office under this name it was to be understood that it was he and that he was to be admitted to all offices of the City, notwithstanding such name. They also decreed that such facts, absolution, declaration, etc. be recorded for perpetual remembrance in the Book of the other laws and provisions. And this decision was passed in the regular Council of the Popolo and the Comune with all the formalities and ceremonies then customary in the ordinances of the people of Florence."

Fig. 10. Portrait of Bartoluccio, Ghiberti's stepfather: Bronze Head on the frame of Ghiberti's first Baptistery Door

Bartolo di Michele orafo, called Bartoluccio, was Ghiberti's stepfather. A few years after the Signoria's decision, Ghiberti signed his second door: LAVRENTII DE CIONIS DE GHIBERTIS. The portrait of his master and putative father appears amongst the heads on his first door (fig. 10).

---

[1] The art critics of the Renaissance used the words *sculpture* and *painting* in a different, more metaphorical sense than we do. This is best explained by a quotation from the *Dialogues* of Francisco de Hollanda: "*I think, said Latanzio, that I heard Francisco de Hollanda just now include among works of painting the tomb [of the Medici in San Lorenzo in Florence] which you, Signor Michelangelo, carved in marble; and I know not how you may give to sculpture the name of painting.—I answered . . . You will find that all professions which have most art, understanding and charm are those akin to the design in painting . . . as sculpture or the carving of statues, which is naught else but the very art of painting . . . In books we find Phidias and Praxiteles celebrated as painters, although we know for certain that they were sculptors in marble. . . . Donatello (the first modern sculptor to deserve fame and renown in Italy) in instructing his pupils used merely to bid them draw and would sum up all his teaching in the phrase: 'My pupils, when I bid you draw I give you the whole art of sculpture'.—*" Though Ghiberti's plaques on his second door could be called *paintings in bronze*, owing to their style which makes pronounced use of light and shade, Vasari, when he called him a painter, was thinking only of paying tribute to the genius of the master.

[2] The name of Ghiberti's father was Lorenzo di Cione di Ser Bonaccorso, his mother's name was Monna Fiore. Cione died in 1406 and Bartolo (or Bartoluccio) married Ghiberti's mother. In 1444, when Ghiberti tried to secure election to the office of the *Dodici Buonuomini*, or Twelve Aldermen, he had to defend himself against a denunciation that he was the illegitimate son of Bartoluccio. Ghiberti's petition went to the Signoria of Florence, and he was acquitted. Baldinucci (1681) tells this story well: "*It now happened that when Lorenzo had in 1443 been elected to the office of the Dodici Buonuomini—one of the three highest which are today known as the Collegio—someone who wished to darken his fame and to oppose the rise of his family lodged with the Magistrato de Conservadori di Legge an information to the following effect: 'Lorenzo di Bartolo, who works on the gates of San Giovanni, elected to the office of the Dodici, is disqualified from holding such office since he was not born in lawful wedlock. For he is the son of Bartolo and of Monna Fiore, his wife or rather his mistress, who was the daughter of a labourer of Val di Sieve and was married at Pelago to one Cione Paltami, a very useless and almost forgotten person, who did not please the said Fiore. So she left him and came to Florence where she chanced to meet the afore-named Bartolo about 1374, from whom she had two children within four or five years, first a girl and later, about 1378, this Lorenzo. Bartolo reared him and taught him his craft, which was that of a goldsmith. The said Cione died about 1406 and when Bartolo had talked to his friends, who made it clear to him that it was sinful to live in adultery, he married Fiore as is well known to all and sundry, and borne out by the documents of the marriage. If Lorenzo calls himself the son of Cione and not of Bartolo, you will find that Cione never had any children from Fiore and that Lorenzo has taken over and used Bartolo's property and has sold and used it like a son and lawful heir. And it was because he knew himself to be disqualified that he has never accepted the office of a Console of this Guild, to which he was elected several times, but for quite trivial reasons has had his name struck out.'* Such was the wording of the denunciation. It was further said that he was incapable of holding such office since he had not paid the taxes for the period prescribed by law, but only for a short while and under the name of the said Bartoluccio; that Cione had never paid them, but that even as son of

[3] No such medals are known. There are, however, portraits of his relatives and friends amongst the small heads on his first and second door.

Romagna. At Rimini⁴ they painted a chamber for the Signor Pandolfo Malatesta, and did many other works which were carefully finished, giving great satisfaction to Pandolfo, who, while still a youth, took great delight in matters of design. Lorenzo, however, continued to pursue his study of design, and to work in relief in wax, stucco, and other like things, knowing that such small reliefs are a sculptor's method of drawing, and that without them it is impossible to attain to perfection.

¶3] He had not been long absent from home when the plague ceased, and the Signoria of Florence and the Guild of the Merchants, seeing that there were a number of excellent artists in sculpture at that time, both foreigners and Florentines, thought that it would be a favourable opportunity to make the other two doors of S. Giovanni, the ancient and principal church of the city, a matter which had frequently been discussed. It was arranged by them that all the masters considered to be the best in Italy should be invited to come to Florence to compete in making bronze panels similar to those which Andrea Pisano had done for the first door⁵. Bartoluccio wrote to inform Lorenzo of this decision, for he was then working at Pesaro, and advised him to return to Florence to show what he could do, that this was an excellent opportunity for him to make his name and to show his ability, in addition to which he might turn the matter to such advantage that neither of them would need to work any longer at making earrings.

¶4] The words of Bartoluccio so moved Lorenzo that, despite the favours heaped upon him by Pandolfo, by the painter, and by all the court, Lorenzo obtained leave from that lord to depart, and bid farewell to the painter, although they were very sorry and reluctant to let him go. Their promises and offers of higher wages availed nothing, for to Lorenzo it seemed worth a thousand years to return to Florence, and he accordingly set out and reached his home in safety. Many foreigners had already arrived and reported themselves to the consuls of the arts. From among them seven masters in all were selected: three Florentines, and the remainder Tuscans. A provision of money was set apart for them, and it was stipulated that within a year each of them should produce, as an example of his skill, a bronze panel of the same size as those of the first door. It was determined that the scene represented should be the sacrifice of Isaac by Abraham, which was considered to be a good subject in which the masters could grapple with the difficulties of the art, because it comprises a landscape, figures both nude and draped, and animals, while the figures in the foreground might be made in full relief, those in the middle distance in half-relief, and those in the background in bas-relief. The competitors for this work were: Filippo di Ser Brunellesco, Donatello⁶ and Lorenzo di Bartoluccio, Florentines, and Jacopo della Quercia of Siena, Niccolò d'Arezzo⁷ his pupil, Francesco di Valdambrino, and Simone da Colle, surnamed *of the bronzes*, who all promised the consuls to have their panels ready at the appointed time. They set to work and devoted all their study and diligence, all their strength and knowledge, to surpass each other, keeping what they did a close secret, so that they might not light upon the same ideas. Lorenzo alone, who enjoyed the help of Bartoluccio, who made him take great pains and prepare many models before he resolved upon adopting any one of them, continually brought his fellow-citizens, and also passing strangers if they understood the trade, to see his work and hear their opinion. By the aid of their criticisms he was enabled to produce a model which was beautifully made and absolutely without a fault. Having shaped his figures and cast the whole in bronze, it proved excellent; and he and his father, Bartoluccio, polished it with such devotion and patience that it was impossible for it to have been better finished. When the time arrived for it to be exhibited in the competition, his panel and those of the other masters were handed over to the Guild of the Merchants to be adjudicated upon. When they came to be examined by the consuls and several other citizens many various opinions were expressed. Numbers of strangers had assembled in Florence, some painters, some sculptors, and some goldsmiths, who were invited by the consuls to come and judge the works in conjunction with others of the same professions who lived in Florence. They numbered thirty-four persons in all, each of them being an adept in his art, and although there were differences of opinion among them, some preferring the style of one and some that of another, yet they were agreed that Filippo di Ser Brunellesco and Lorenzo di Bartoluccio had composed and finished a larger number of figures better than Donatello had done, although his panel exhibited great powers of design. In that of Jacopo della Quercia the figures were good but lacking in delicacy, in spite of the good design and the care

bestowed. The work of Francesco di Valdambrino contained good heads and was well finished, but the composition was confused. That of Simone da Colle was a good cast, because he was a founder by profession, but the design was not very good. The production of Niccolò d'Arezzo, showing great skill, was marred by stunted figures and absence of finish. Lorenzo's alone was perfect in every part, and it may still be seen in the audience chamber of the Guild of the Merchants. The whole scene was well designed and the composition excellent, the figures being slender and graceful, the pose admirable and so beautifully finished that it did not look as if it had been cast and polished, but rather as if it had been created by a breath. Donatello and Filippo, when they perceived what diligence Lorenzo had devoted to his work, withdrew to one side and agreed that the work ought to be given to him, for it seemed to them that public and private interests would thus be best served, and as Lorenzo was a young man, not past twenty, he would be able to realize in the production of this work the great promise of his beautiful scene, which, according to their judgement, he had made more excellently than the others, adding that it would be more shameful to dispute his right to pre-eminence than generous to admit it.

¶5] Accordingly Lorenzo began on that door opposite the *opera* of S. Giovanni, constructing a large wooden frame for a part of it of the exact size he desired, in the shape of a frame with the ornamentation of heads at the angles about the spaces for containing the scenes and the surrounding friezes. After he had made the mould and dried it with all diligence, he set up a huge furnace, which I remember having seen, and there cast the frame in metal. He did this in some premises he had bought opposite S. Maria Nuova, where the hospital of the weavers, known as the Threshing-floor, now stands. But realizing that the cast did not come out well, he did not lose courage or become distracted, but traced the cause of the disorder and altered his mould with great quickness ⟨without anyone knowing it, recasting the work, which came out most successfully.

¶6] He went on similarly with the rest of the work, casting each scene separately, and then putting them in their appointed places. The division of the scenes was similar to that adopted by Andrea Pisano in the first door designed for him by Giotto. He represented twenty scenes from the New Testament, and beneath these he left eight spaces. Beginning from the bottom he made the four Evangelists, two on each door, and the four Doctors of the Church, similarly arranged, differing from each other in their attitudes and draperies, one writing, one reading, the others reflecting, and in their varied expressions they are very life-like and excellently made. In the framework about the scenes is a border of ivy leaves and other things, which are set in the framework, and at each corner is the head of a man or a woman in full relief, representing prophets and sibyls, all very good in their variety, and displaying the excellence of Lorenzo's genius.

¶7] Above the Doctors and Evangelists already mentioned, beginning from the bottom on the side nearest S. Maria del Fiore, there are four pictures, the first an Annunciation, in which the attitude of the Virgin exhibits terror and sudden fear as she gracefully turns herself at the coming of the angel. Next to this he made the Nativity, Our Lady lying down and resting while Joseph is contemplating, also shepherds and angels who are singing. On the other side from this, and on the other part of the door, but on the same level, is the story of the coming of the Magi and adoration of Christ, giving Him tribute, comprising the court which followed them with horses and equipments, made with great skill. Next to this is Christ disputing in the Temple with the doctors, where the wonder and attention of the doctors who are listening to Him are no less finely expressed than the joy of Mary and Joseph at finding Him again. Returning to the other end, over the Annunciation is the scene of the Baptism of Christ in the Jordan by John, the postures of the figures exhibiting the reverence of the one and the faith of the other. Beside this is the Temptation of Christ by the devil, who is terrified by the words of Jesus, and is in an attitude expressive of his fear, recognizing that He is the Son of God. Next to this, on the other part, is Christ driving out the changers from the Temple, overthrowing their money, victims for sacrifice, doves, and other merchandise, where the figures of some men who are falling over each other in their flight are very graceful and well imagined. Next to this Lorenzo put the shipwreck of the Apostles, where Peter leaves the boat and is sinking in the water, while Christ upholds him. This scene is remarkable for the varied attitudes of the Apostles who are at work in the ship, and the faith of Peter is expressed by his coming towards Christ. Returning to the other end once again, over the Baptism is the Transfiguration on Mount Tabor, where Lorenzo expresses in the attitude of the Apostles the bedazzlement experienced by mortal eyes at the heavenly vision; Christ is displayed in His divinity between Moses and Elias, holding His head high and His arms open. Beside this is the Raising of Lazarus, who emerges from the tomb bound hand and foot, and stands upright to the astonishment of the spectators. Martha is there and Mary Magdalene, who is kissing the feet of the Lord with the utmost humility and reverence. Next to this, on the other part, is the Entry into Jerusalem on an ass, while the children of the

---

⁴ See note 5 to Ghiberti's Autobiography.

⁵ Fig. 13.

⁶ Donatello's year of birth is not known for certain; it may be that he was born as early as 1382. If he had a share in this competition, it was probably as an assistant of Brunelleschi.

⁷ Ghiberti has two Niccolòs in his list of the competitors: the goldsmith Niccolò di Luca Spinelli of Arezzo, and Niccolò di Piero Lamberti of Florence, who till 1415 worked on the Porta della Mandorla etc. in Florence, and afterwards in Venice and Bologna.

Hebrews, in varied attitudes, throw down their garments, olive branches and palms, and the Apostles are following the Saviour. Beside this is a very fine Last Supper very well arranged, as the Apostles are seated round a long table, half of them being on one side and half on the other. Over the Transfiguration he made the Agony in the Garden, where the three Apostles may be observed sleeping in various attitudes. Next to this is Christ receiving the kiss of Judas, where there are many noteworthy things, the Apostles running away, and the Jews represented as taking Christ, with great vigour. On the other part is Christ bound to the column, His face somewhat distorted with the pain of the scourging and in a compassionate attitude, while the Jews who are scourging Him show their terrible rage and vindictive feeling. Following this is the scene when He is brought before Pilate, who washes his hands and sentences Him to the cross. Over the Agony in the Garden and in the last row of scenes is Christ carrying the cross and going to His death, led by a fierce band of soldiers who are dragging Him along with rough gestures. Grief and weeping are expressed in the gestures of the Maries, so that had one been present it would not have been possible to realize the scene better. Besides this Lorenzo made Christ on the cross, with Our Lady and St John the Evangelist seated on the ground in attitudes full of grief and indignation. Next to this, on the other part, is the Resurrection, the guards overcome by the thunder stand like dead men, while Christ is ascending in an attitude which has all the attributes of glorification in the perfection of His beautiful members, created by the skilful industry of Lorenzo. The last space contains the Coming of the Holy Spirit, the attitudes and expectancy of those who receive it being exquisite. No time or labour was spared to make the work perfect. The limbs of the nude figures are most beautiful in every part, and although the draperies still possess something of the old-fashioned style of Giotto, yet the general tendency is towards the modern manner, and figures of this particular size possess a certain delicate gracefulness. In fine, the composition of the various scenes is so well managed that it deserves the praise bestowed on it in the commencement by Filippo Brunelleschi, and even more. From his fellow-citizens Lorenzo obtained the most complete recognition of his labours, and won the highest praise from them and from all artists, both native and foreign. The entire work cost 22,000 florins, including the outside ornamentation, which is also of metal, and the festoons of fruit and animals carved there. The metal doors weighed 34,000 pounds.

¶8] When the work was completed, the consuls of the Guild of the Merchants felt that they had been very well served; and, as everyone praised Lorenzo, they proposed that he should make a bronze statue four and a half braccia high in memory of St John the Baptist for the exterior of Or San Michele, in the niche belonging to the cloth dressers. Accordingly he began this, and never rested until he had finished it. The work has been much admired, and the artist put his name to it on the hem of the robe; it was set up in the year 1414, and shows an approach towards the good modern style in the head, in an arm, which looks as if it was actual flesh, and in the hands and the whole attitude of the figure. He was the first to begin to imitate the masterpieces of the ancient Romans, studying them very carefully, as everyone should who wishes to become a good craftsman. For the front he made an experiment in mosaic, introducing a half-figure of a prophet.

¶9] Lorenzo's fame had already spread through all Italy and beyond as the most skilful modern founder. Accordingly, when Jacopo dalla Fonte[8] and Vecchietta of Siena and Donatello were required to decorate the baptistery of S. Giovanni with some scenes and figures in bronze,[9] and as the Sienese had seen Lorenzo's work in Florence, they negotiated with him and employed him to make two scenes of the life of St John the Baptist. One of them is the Baptism of Christ, comprising a quantity of nude and draped figures, very richly wrought, and the other St John before Herod. In these scenes Lorenzo surpassed and vanquished the other artists there, and accordingly he received great praise from the Sienese and from others who saw them.

¶10] The masters of the mint at Florence had to make a statue for one of the niches outside Or San Michele, opposite the Guild of Wool, which was to be a St Matthew of the same height as the St John mentioned above. They allotted the task to Lorenzo, who executed it to perfection, and received more praise for it than for his St John, because it was more modern in style.

¶11] This induced the consuls of the Guild of Wool to propose that he should make another statue, also of bronze, in the next niche, which should be of the same size as the others, and represent their patron, St Stephen. This he also completed, giving a fine polish to the bronze, so that it afforded no less satisfaction than his other works.

¶12] At this time Maestro Leonardo Dati was general of the Friar Preachers, and in order to leave a memorial of himself to his native place, in S. Maria Novella, where he had professed, he employed

Lorenzo to make a bronze tomb with his own effigy in the attitude of death. The praise accorded to this work led to Lorenzo being employed to make one in S. Croce for Lodovico degli Albizzi and another for Niccolò Valori.[10]

¶13] After these things Cosimo and Lorenzo de'Medici, wishing to honour the bodies and relics of the three martyrs Protus, Hyacinth and Nemesius, had them fetched from Casentino, where they had remained for many years in slight esteem, and employed Lorenzo to make a metal shrine, in the middle of which are two angels in bas-relief, holding a garland of olive branches encircling the names of the martyrs. The relics were deposited in this shrine, and placed in the church of the monastery of the Angeli at Florence, with these words[11] carved in marble on the side towards the church of the monks: *Clarissimi viri Cosmas et Laurentius fratres neglectas diu Sanctorum reliquias martyrum religioso studio ac fidelissima pietate suis sumptibus aereis loculis condendas colendasque curarunt.*[11] On the outer side, where the little church faces the street, are these words carved in the marble beneath a coat of arms with the balls: *Hic condita sunt corpora sanctorum (Christi) martyrum Proti et Hyacinthi et Nemesii. Ann. Dom. MCCCCXXVIII.*

¶14] This having proved so successful, the wardens of S. Maria del Fiore became desirous of having a sarcophagus and tomb of metal constructed to receive the body of St Zenobius, bishop of Florence, of the dimensions of three and a half braccia by two. Besides the decoration of divers ornaments, Lorenzo made a scene on the body of the tomb representing the incident where the saint raises the child left in his custody by its mother, and who had died during her absence on a pilgrimage. The second scene is of another child, killed by a cart and raised by the saint, who also raises one of the two servants sent to him by St Ambrose, who was left dead on the Alps, the other sorrowing in the presence of St Zenobius, who is comforting him and saying, *He is only sleeping; go and you will find him alive.* At the back are six small angels, holding a garland of elm leaves, on which are carved some sentences in praise of the saint.

¶15] While the works of Lorenzo were increasing his reputation every day, and he was engaged upon work in silver and gold as well as bronze for numberless individuals, there came into the possession of Giovanni, the son of Cosimo de'Medici,[12] a large cornelian carved with the flaying of Marsyas by Apollo. It was said to have been used by the Emperor Nero as a seal. As the stone was large, and very valuable for its size and the wonderful carving on it, Giovanni gave it to Lorenzo to make a mount of wrought gold for it. The artist laboured at it for many months, surrounding this beautiful work with a carved ornamentation no less perfect than the carving on the stone itself.

¶16] This event led him to do many more things in gold and silver, which are no longer to be found. For Pope Martin (V) he made a gold fastening for his cope, with figures in full relief and jewels of great price among them, a most excellent piece of work. He also made a mitre, marvellously chased with gold leaves and many small figures in full relief in the midst, which was considered very beautiful, and besides the fame which he acquired he benefited considerably owing to the liberality of the Pope.

¶17] In the year 1439[13] Pope Eugenius (IV) came to Florence to unite the Greek and Latin churches and to hold a Council. When he saw Lorenzo's works he was equally delighted with them and with the artist himself. Accordingly he employed Lorenzo to make a gold mitre for him, weighing fifteen pounds, with pearls weighing five and a half pounds, the whole, including the jewels, being valued at 30,000 gold ducats. It is said that there were six pearls like filbert nuts, and it is impossible to imagine the curious beauty of the setting of the jewels in a variety of children and other figures, forming a very graceful ornamentation as shown by the design for it. For this work Lorenzo received most hearty thanks from the pontiff for himself and his friends, besides the first payment.

¶18] Florence had acquired such celebrity by the works of the most ingenious artist that the consuls of the Guild of the Merchants determined to assign to him the third door of S. Giovanni, to be likewise made in metal. In the case of the first door Lorenzo had, by their direction, carried out the ornamentation which surrounds the figures and binds together the framework, like that of Andrea Pisano. But now the consuls, recognizing how greatly Lorenzo had excelled him, resolved to move the middle door, which was Andrea's, and to put it up opposite the Misericordia, and to employ Lorenzo to make new

---

[8] Jacopo della Quercia.

[9] Vecchietta, born in 1412, had no share in this work; but Vasari forgets to mention Ghiberti's two friends, Turini and Goro di Ser Neroccio, who contributed bronzes to the font.

[10] Vasari's mistake for Lodovico degli *Obizzi* and *Bartolommeo* Valori.

[11] The inscription has disappeared. This is the only authenticated work of Ghiberti which is no longer at the place for which it was made—it is now at the Museo Nazionale del Bargello in Florence.

[12] This work of setting was done by Ghiberti at the latest in 1429. In this year Giovanni di Cosimo de' Medici was only eight years old. Vasari may be confusing him with the father of Cosimo, Giovanni di Averardo, who died in 1429.

[13] Eugenius IV visited Florence for the first time as early as 1434. I assume that Ghiberti worked for him in 1436, in which year the Pope consecrated the Cathedral of Florence. In 1439 the Council of Basle deposed Eugenius IV and elected Amadeus of Savoy as Felix V; Eugenius returned to Florence, but found the general feeling against himself; he resided there, however, till March, 1443.

doors for the middle, judging that he would devote his utmost energies to the task. They left the whole matter in his hands, saying that they gave him full liberty to do as he pleased and that he should make it as ornamental, rich, perfect and beautiful as he possibly could, or as could be imagined, without regard to time or expense, and that as he had surpassed all the other figure-makers up to that time, he should in this work surpass himself.

¶19] Lorenzo began his task, lavishing upon it the very best of his powers. He divided the door into ten squares, five on each side, the spaces left for the scenes being a braccia and a third in size. In the ornamentation of the framework surrounding the scenes are upright niches containing figures in almost full relief to the number of twenty, and all very beautiful, such as a nude Samson[14] embracing a column and holding a jaw-bone in his hand, displaying the highest degree of perfection attained by the ancients in their figures of Hercules, whether of bronze or of marble; as does a Joshua who is in the act of speaking to his army.[15] Besides these, there are many prophets and sibyls dressed in various styles of draperies, and with varied arrangements of their heads, hair and other ornaments, as well as twelve recumbent figures[16] in the niches in the transverse parts of the frame. At the corners he made circles containing heads of women, youths and old men, to the number of thirty-four,[17] introducing his own portrait in the middle of the door, near the place where he has inscribed his name.[18] The older man beside him is his father, Bartoluccio.[19] In addition to the heads he made foliage, mouldings and other ornaments with the greatest mastery.

¶20] The scenes represented on this door are taken from the Old Testament.[20]

¶21] There is also the ornamentation of the architraves which surround the door, made up of fruit and festoons of the same high level of excellence.

¶22] The entire work, in detail and as a whole, is a striking example of what may be accomplished by the skill and energy of a sculptor-artist in dealing with figures, some practically in relief, some in half-relief, and some in bas-relief, in invention and the composition of figures, and in the striking attitudes of the women and men, the variety of the buildings, the perspectives, the graceful comportment of both sexes, with a well-regulated sense of decorum, gravity in the old and lightness and grace in the young. Indeed, the doors may be said to be perfect in every particular, the finest masterpiece in the world whether among the ancients or the moderns. Right well does Lorenzo merit praise, for one day Michelagnolo Buonarroti stopped to look at these doors, and on being asked his opinion he said, *They are so fine that they might fittingly stand at the entrance of Paradise,* a truly noble encomium pronounced by one well able to judge.[21] Lorenzo certainly deserved his success, for he began them at the age of twenty and laboured at them with more than ordinary exertion for over forty years.

¶23] In polishing and cleaning this work after it was cast Lorenzo was assisted by many youths who afterwards became famous masters, such as Filippo Brunelleschi, Masolino da Panicale,[22] Niccolò Lamberti, goldsmiths, Parri Spinelli, Antonio Filarete, Paolo Uccello, Antonio del Pollaiuolo, then quite young, and by many others who were engaged together upon the same task, and by means of this association and mutual conference they benefited themselves no less than Lorenzo. Besides the payment which Lorenzo received from the consuls, the Signoria gave him a considerable property near the abbey of Settimo, and it was not long before he was admitted to the Signoria and thus received the honour of entering the chief magistracy of the city.

¶24] After this stupendous work, Lorenzo made the bronze ornamentation for the door of the same church which is opposite the Misericordia, introducing his marvellous foliage, but was unable to finish this on account of his unexpected death, after he had arranged everything and all but finished the model for the reconstruction of that door which Andrea Pisano had made. This model has fared badly in these days, but I saw it when I was a young man in the Borgo Allegri before it had been allowed to go to ruin by Lorenzo's descendants.

---

[14] Plate 89.

[15] In the pose of a Roman orator; but the figure probably represents David (plate 86).

[16] There are only four recumbent figures.

[17] Only twenty-four heads.

[18] Plate 1. [19] Plate 79; but see the note on plate 1.

[20] Vasari's detailed description of the second door is omitted here as it is, on the whole, but a repetition of what Ghiberti himself says about it (Autobiography ¶16). Some other short passages are also left out as being of too little importance.

[21] This famous saying, quoted in every book and article on Ghiberti, may have a very local meaning (as Paul Schubring was the first to suspect); *Paradiso* was originally the name of the Loggia connecting the old Cathedral, S. Reparata, with the Baptistery. If so, Michelangelo may just have meant that Ghiberti's second door was worthy to stand in this central place of Florence, facing the Cathedral.

[22] Masolino da Panicale is probably confused here with the stonemason Maso di Cristofano; Niccolò Lamberti, who at this time was not in Florence (see note 7), is probably confused with Niccolò Spinelli, and the latter may be identical with the following Parri Spinelli (to whom Berenson attributed several drawings; see also Sirén, Essentials in Art, 1920, p. 129f.).

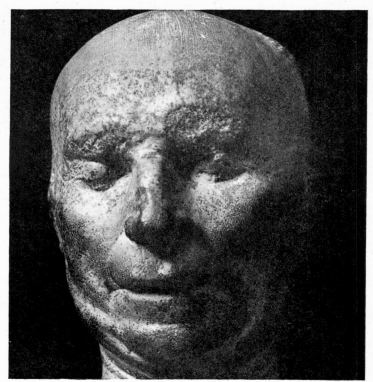

Fig. 11. Death Mask of Brunelleschi. 1446.
Florence, Museo dell' Opera del Duomo

¶25] Lorenzo, besides works by his own hand, bequeathed to his heirs many antiques of marble and of bronze, such as the bed of Polycletus, which was a rare treasure, a bronze leg of life-size, and some heads of women and men, with a quantity of vases, for which he had sent to Greece at a great expense. He also left some torsos and many other things, which were dissipated like his property, some being sold to M. Giovanni Gaddi, sometime clerk of the chamber. Among these was the bed of Polycletus and the other more valuable articles.[23]

¶26] Lorenzo took an interest in many things and delighted in painting on glass. In S. Maria del Fiore he made the circular windows round the cupola, except one by the hand of Donatello, representing Christ crowning the Virgin. Lorenzo also made the three rose-windows over the principal door of the same church, and all those of the chapels and the tribunes, as well as that in the façade of S. Croce. In Arezzo he made a window for the principal chapel of the Pieve, representing a Coronation of the Virgin,[24] and two other figures for Lazzaro di Feo di Baccio, a wealthy merchant. But as all these were made of highly coloured Venetian glass they rather darken the places where they are placed.

¶27] Lorenzo was appointed to be the associate of Brunellesco when the latter was charged with the construction of the cupola of S. Maria del Fiore, but was afterwards removed.

¶28] Lorenzo wrote a work in the vulgar tongue treating of many things, but so that little profit can be derived from it. The only good thing that it contains, in my opinion, comes after the description of the ancient painters, particularly those cited by Pliny, where he makes a brief mention of Cimabue, Giotto, and many others of that time, and he has treated this much more briefly than he should, and that for no better reason than to discourse at length about himself and to describe minutely one by one the works which he produced.

¶29] Having at length attained the sixty-fourth year[25] of his life, he was attacked by a violent and continuous fever and died, leaving an immortal fame in his works and in the descriptions of writers. He was buried honourably in S. Croce. His portrait is on the principal door of S. Giovanni, in the middle border when the door is shut, being represented as bald, his father, Bartoluccio, being next him, and near them the following words may be read: LAVRENTII CIONIS DE GHIBERTIS MIRA ARTE FABRICATVM.

¶30] Lorenzo's designs were excellent and made with great relief, as may be seen in our book of designs, in an Evangelist by his hand, and some other very fine works in chiaroscuro. Bartoluccio, his father, also designed very fairly, as is shown by another Evangelist by his hand in the same book, though perceptibly inferior to Lorenzo's. I had these designs, together with some by Giotto, from Vettorio Ghiberti[26] in the year 1528, while I was still quite young, and I have always valued them highly.

---

[23] See Schlosser, p. 123f. on Ghiberti's collection of antiques.—Also C. Frey's edition of *Codice Magliabechiano*, 1892, pp. 148-150.

[24] The stained glass windows in Arezzo have been lost.

[25] Ghiberti died at the age of seventy-seven.

[26] A great-grandson of Ghiberti; painter and sculptor, 1501-42.

BIBLIOGRAPHICAL NOTE

ALL the books and articles which to my mind are worth mentioning are quoted in my notes to Ghiberti's Autobiography, the Vasari Vita and the Notes on the Plates. Some titles are given only once in full and later on in abbreviated form ; namely :

Wilhelm von Bode, *Florentiner Bildhauer der Renaissance,* 4th edition, Berlin 1921 (= Bode) ;

Oskar Wulff, *Ghibertis Entwicklung im Madonnen-Relief,* in *Amtliche Berichte, Beiblatt zum Berliner Jahrbuch,* XLIII, 9-10, September and October, 1922, pp. 91-103 (= Wulff);

Julius von Schlosser, *Leben und Meinungen des Florentiner Bildners Lorenzo Ghiberti,* Basel 1941 (= Schlosser).

In addition to Schlosser's standard book on Ghiberti, there are two other monographs on the master: *Ghiberti et son école,* by Charles Perkins, Director of the Boston Museum, Paris 1886 (published only in French), and *Lorenzo Ghiberti,* by Leo Planiscig, Vienna 1940. The earliest XIXth-century appreciations of Ghiberti are those in L. Cicognara's *Storia della scultura dal suo risorgimento in Italia,* Prato 1823 f. and in C. Fr. von Rumohr's *Italienische Forschungen,* part II, 1827-31.

The best edition of the Vasari Biography is that by Karl Frey : *Vita di Lorenzo Ghiberti scultore Fiorentino, scritta da Giorgio Vasari, con i Commentarii di Lorenzo Ghiberti,* Berlin 1886 ; cf. *Gelli,* ed. Mancini, in *Archivio storico italiano,* s.v., vol. XVII, 1896, pp. 34-62.

Besides the two slender volumes by Schmarsow (quoted in my notes), there are four other studies on Ghiberti's style, but they will not be to everybody's taste : Bertha Friedmann, *Ghibertis Verhältnis zur Gothik und Renaissance,* Leipzig 1913 ; Hedwig Gollob, *Lorenzo Ghibertis künstlerischer Werdegang* (Zur Kunstgeschichte des Auslandes, Heft 126), Strasbourg 1929 ; Lionello Venturi, in *L'Arte,* 1923 (also in *Pretesti di Critica,* Milan 1928, p. 95 f.) ; and Adrian Stokes in his *The Quattro Cento, A different Conception of the Italian Renaissance,* London, 1932, pp. 85-98.

Extensive bibliographies are to be found in F. Schottmüllers' article in *Thieme-Becker's Künstler-Lexikon:* " Ghiberti ", Leipzig 1920, vol. XIII ; and in Lionello Venturi's article in the *Enciclopedia italiana* XVI, 1932 ; a few bibliographical additions in Schlosser's *Ghiberti,* 1941, pp. 119-120.

Reproductions of Ghiberti's sculptures and those of his period, are found most easily in Wilhelm von Bode's *Denkmäler der Renaissance-Skulptur Toskanas,* Munich 1892-95.

The best survey of all editions of Ghiberti's own writings and of the criticism on them, is given in Julius von Schlosser's *Die Kunstliteratur,* Vienna 1924, pp. 87-91, and in Filippo Rossi's translation of that book, *La Letteratura artistica,* Florence 1935. Compare also Schlosser's *Künstlerprobleme der Frührenaissance,* V, *Lorenzo Ghiberti,* in *Sitzungsberichte der philosophisch-historischen Klasse der Wiener Akademie,* Vienna 1934. A complete facsimile of Ghiberti's second *commentarius,* including the manuscript of the autobiography, is printed in Julius von Schlosser's *Prolegomena zu einer künftigen Ausgabe der Commentarii,* in *Jahrbuch der Zentralkommission fur Kunst- und historischen Denkmäler,* Vienna 1910, pp. 105 f.

THE PLATES

CORRIGENDA:

Plate 79. Read: *probably his son Vittorio*

Plate 112. Read: *Tribuna di Zanobi* (not Zenobi)

Plate 119. Add: *enlarged reproduction*

Plate 129. Read: *1424-32* (not 1405)

1. GHIBERTI'S SELF-PORTRAIT. BRONZE. FROM THE SECOND DOOR OF THE BAPTISTERY AT FLORENCE. ABOUT 1444-48. (ENLARGED REPRODUCTION—CF. NOS. 41 AND 45)

2. FILIPPO BRUNELLESCHI: THE SACRIFICE OF ISAAC. BRONZE RELIEF, MADE IN COMPETITION FOR THE NORTH DOOR OF THE BAPTISTERY. 1401. FLORENCE, BARGELLO

3. LORENZO GHIBERTI: THE SACRIFICE OF ISAAC.   BRONZE RELIEF, MADE IN COMPETITION FOR THE NORTH DOOR OF THE
BAPTISTERY. 1401. FLORENCE, BARGELLO

4. GHIBERTI'S FIRST DOOR OF THE BAPTISTERY AT FLORENCE. 1403–24. BRONZE. THE NORTH DOOR
(SURMOUNTED BY FRANCESCO RUSTICI'S BRONZE GROUP "THE PREACHING OF THE BAPTIST", 1511)

5. THE NORTH DOOR OF THE BAPTISTERY AT FLORENCE. BRONZE. 1403–24.
WITH TWENTY SCENES FROM THE LIFE OF CHRIST; THE FOUR EVANGELISTS, AND FOUR DOCTORS OF THE CHURCH

6. ANNUNCIATION. PANEL OF THE FIRST DOOR OF THE BAPTISTERY AT FLORENCE (CF. NO. 5)

7. ADORATION OF THE MAGI. PANEL OF THE FIRST DOOR OF THE BAPTISTERY AT FLORENCE (CF. NO. 5)

8. CHRIST IN THE TEMPLE. PANEL OF THE FIRST DOOR OF THE BAPTISTERY AT FLORENCE (CF. NO. 5)

9. THE TEMPTATION. PANEL OF THE FIRST DOOR OF THE BAPTISTERY AT FLORENCE (CF. NO. 5)

10. THE STORM ON THE LAKE OF GALILEE. PANEL OF THE FIRST DOOR OF THE BAPTISTERY AT FLORENCE (CF. NO. 5)

11. THE TRANSFIGURATION. PANEL OF THE FIRST DOOR OF THE BAPTISTERY AT FLORENCE (CF. NO. 5)

12. THE RAISING OF LAZARUS   PANEL OF THE FIRST DOOR OF THE BAPTISTERY AT FLORENCE (CF. NO. 5)

13. THE ENTRY INTO JERUSALEM. PANEL OF THE FIRST DOOR OF THE BAPTISTERY AT FLORENCE (CF. NO. 5)

14. THE SCOURGING OF CHRIST. PANEL OF THE FIRST DOOR OF THE BAPTISTERY AT FLORENCE (CF. NO. 5)

15. THE ROAD TO CALVARY. PANEL OF THE FIRST DOOR OF THE BAPTISTERY AT FLORENCE (CF. NO. 5)

16. PENTECOST. PANEL OF THE FIRST DOOR OF THE BAPTISTERY AT FLORENCE (CF. NO. 5)

17. THE BAPTISM OF CHRIST.
DETAIL OF NO. 5

18. PILATE WASHING HIS HANDS.
DETAIL OF NO. 5

19. THE RAISING OF LAZARUS. DETAIL OF NO. 12

20. CHRIST ENTERING JERUSALEM. DETAIL OF NO. 13

21. CHRIST DRIVING THE TRADERS FROM THE TEMPLE. DETAIL OF NO. 5

22–26. DETAILS OF THE DECORATED BORDERS FRAMING THE PANELS OF THE FIRST DOOR (CF. NO. 5)

27–32. SIX PANELS OF
THE FIRST DOOR

(27) THE NATIVITY

(28) THE AGONY IN THE
GARDEN

(29) THE LAST SUPPER

(30) THE BETRAYAL OF
CHRIST

(31) THE CRUCIFIXION

(32) THE RESURRECTION

33–38. SIX PANELS OF
THE FIRST DOOR

THREE EVANGELISTS AND
THREE DOCTORS OF THE
CHURCH: ST LUKE,
ST MARK, ST MATTHEW;
ST AUGUSTINE, ST JEROME,
ST AMBROSE.

39. ST JOHN THE EVANGELIST. PANEL OF THE FIRST DOOR OF THE BAPTISTERY AT FLORENCE (CF. NO. 5)

40. ST GREGORY THE GREAT. PANEL OF THE FIRST DOOR OF THE BAPTISTERY AT FLORENCE
(CF. NO. 5)

41. GHIBERTI'S SELF-PORTRAIT. ABOUT 1420. TWO VIEWS OF THE SMALL BRONZE HEAD ON THE FIRST DOOR OF THE BAPTISTERY AT FLORENCE (CF. NOS. 1 AND 5)

42. SMALL BRONZE HEAD ON THE FIRST DOOR OF THE BAPTISTERY AT FLORENCE
(ENLARGED REPRODUCTION—CF. NO. 5)

43. SMALL BRONZE HEAD ON THE FIRST DOOR OF THE BAPTISTERY AT FLORENCE
(ENLARGED REPRODUCTION—CF. NO. 5)

44. SMALL BRONZE HEAD ON THE FIRST DOOR OF THE BAPTISTERY AT FLORENCE
(ENLARGED REPRODUCTION—CF. NO. 5)

45. GHIBERTI'S SECOND DOOR OF THE BAPTISTERY IN FLORENCE. 1425-52. BRONZE. THE EAST DOOR; CALLED "THE GATE OF PARADISE". WITH TEN SCENES FROM THE OLD TESTAMENT

46. CREATION AND FALL OF MAN. PANEL OF THE SECOND DOOR OF THE BAPTISTERY AT FLORENCE (CF. NO. 45)

47. THE CREATOR. DETAIL OF NO. 46

48. CREATION OF EVE. DETAIL OF NO. 46

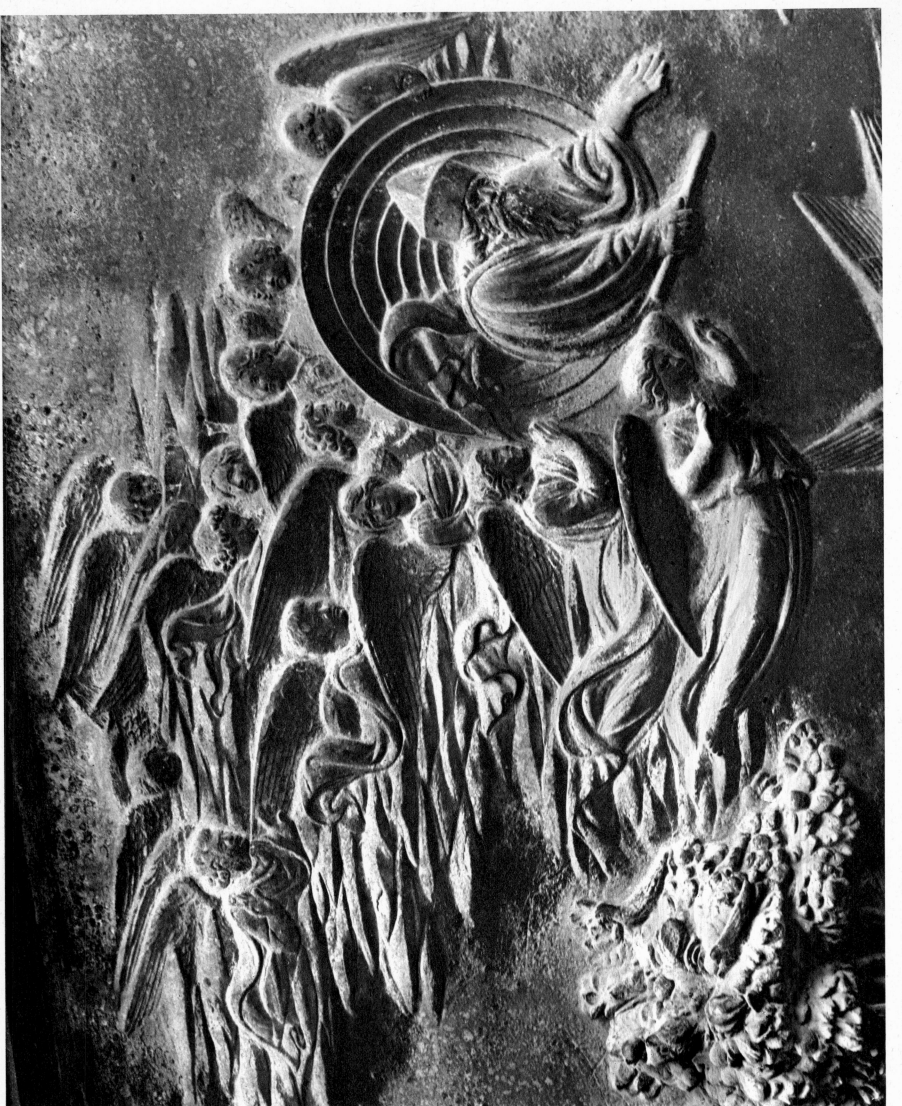

49. THE CREATOR IN A CLOUD OF ANGELS. DETAIL OF NO. 46

51. CAIN AND ABEL. PANEL OF THE SECOND DOOR OF THE BAPTISTERY AT FLORENCE (CF. NO. 45)

52. THE STORY OF NOAH. PANEL OF THE SECOND DOOR OF THE BAPTISTERY AT FLORENCE (CF. NO. 45)

53. THE DRUNKENNESS OF NOAH. DETAIL OF NO. 52

55. STORY OF ABRAHAM. PANEL OF THE SECOND DOOR OF THE BAPTISTERY AT FLORENCE (CF. NOS. 50 AND 3)

56. THE ANGELS VISIT ABRAHAM. DETAIL OF NO. 55

57. JACOB AND ESAU. PANEL OF THE SECOND DOOR OF THE BAPTISTERY AT FLORENCE (CF. NO. 45)

58. REBECCA AND HER COMPANIONS. DETAIL OF NO. 57

59. ISAAC BLESSING JACOB; IN THE BACKGROUND ESAU WITH HIS BOW. DETAIL OF NO. 57

60. ISAAC AND ESAU. DETAIL OF NO. 57

61. THE STORY OF JOSEPH. PANEL OF THE SECOND DOOR OF THE BAPTISTERY AT FLORENCE (CF. NO. 45)

62. THE GOLD CUP FOUND IN BENJAMIN'S SACK. DETAIL OF NO. 61

63. JOSEPH RECOGNIZED BY HIS BRETHREN, AND THE STORY OF BENJAMIN. DETAIL OF NO. 61

64. JOSEPH'S BRETHREN, BRINGING CORN FROM EGYPT. DETAIL OF NO. 61

65. MOSES ON MOUNT SINAI. PANEL OF THE SECOND DOOR OF THE BAPTISTERY AT FLORENCE (CF. NO. 45)

66. THE FRIGHTENED CROWD. DETAIL OF NO. 65

67. JOSHUA CROSSING THE JORDAN AND BESIEGING JERICHO. PANEL OF THE SECOND DOOR OF THE BAPTISTERY AT FLORENCE (CF. NO. 45)

68. PROCESSION OF THE ARK OF THE COVENANT. DETAIL OF NO. 67

69. DAVID AND GOLIATH. PANEL OF THE SECOND DOOR OF THE BAPTISTERY AT FLORENCE (CF. NO. 45)

70. DAVID RETURNING TO JERUSALEM WITH THE HEAD OF GOLIATH. DETAIL OF NO. 69

71. THE MEETING OF SOLOMON AND THE QUEEN OF SHEBA. PANEL OF THE SECOND DOOR OF THE BAPTISTERY AT FLORENCE (CF. NO. 45)

72. SOLOMON AND THE QUEEN OF SHEBA IN THE TEMPLE OF JERUSALEM. DETAIL OF NO. 71

73. SEVEN DETAILS FROM THE DECORATIONS OF THE SECOND DOOR (CF. NO. 45)
(A) THE UPPER BORDER   (B) DETAILS FROM THE OUTSIDE FRAME   (C) RACHEL   (D) AMOS
(E) SAMSON   (F) NOAH

74. OWL. DETAIL FROM THE FRIEZE OF THE SECOND DOOR OF THE BAPTISTERY AT FLORENCE (CF. NO. 45)

75. QUAIL. DETAIL FROM THE FRIEZE OF THE SECOND DOOR OF BAPTISTERY AT FLORENCE (CF. NO. 45)

76. SQUIRREL. DETAIL FROM THE FRIEZE OF THE SECOND DOOR OF THE BAPTISTERY AT FLORENCE (CF. NO. 45)

77. FLOWERS. DETAIL FROM THE FRIEZE OF THE SECOND DOOR OF THE BAPTISTERY AT FLORENCE (CF. NO. 45)

78. FOLIAGE. BRONZE DECORATION ON THE JAMBS OF THE SECOND DOOR OF THE BAPTISTERY AT FLORENCE (CF. NO. 45)

79. PORTRAIT OF AN ASSISTANT OF GHIBERTI. PROBABLY EITHER HIS STEPFATHER, BARTOLUCCIO, OR HIS SON, VITTORIO. SMALL BRONZE
HEAD ON THE SECOND DOOR OF THE BAPTISTERY AT FLORENCE (ENLARGED REPRODUCTION—CF. NO. 45)

80. SMALL BRONZE HEAD ON THE SECOND DOOR OF THE BAPTISTERY AT FLORENCE (ENLARGED REPRODUCTION—CF. NO. 45)

81. SMALL BRONZE HEAD ON THE SECOND DOOR OF THE BAPTISTERY AT FLORENCE (ENLARGED REPRODUCTION—CF. NO. 45)

82. SMALL BRONZE HEAD ON THE SECOND DOOR OF THE BAPTISTERY AT FLORENCE
(ENLARGED REPRODUCTION—CF. NO. 45)

83—85. NOAH'S WIFE, EVE, ADAM. THREE OF THE RECLINING BRONZE FIGURES AT THE ENDS OF THE SECOND DOOR OF THE BAPTISTERY AT FLORENCE (CF. NO. 45)

86—87. DAVID AND JUDITH. BRONZE STATUETTES IN NICHES OF THE SECOND DOOR OF THE BAPTISTERY AT FLORENCE (CF. NO. 45)

88. MIRIAM. BRONZE STATUETTE IN A NICHE OF THE SECOND DOOR OF THE BAPTISTERY AT FLORENCE (CF. NO. 45)

89. SAMSON. BRONZE STATUETTE IN A NICHE OF THE SECOND DOOR OF THE BAPTISTERY AT FLORENCE (CF. NO. 45)

90—93. SAUL, JOSHUA, ISAIAH, JEREMIAH. FOUR BRONZE STATUETTES IN NICHES OF THE SECOND DOOR OF THE BAPTISTERY AT FLORENCE (CF. NO. 45)

94—97. PROPHETS AND WOMEN OF THE BIBLE. FOUR BRONZE STATUETTES IN NICHES OF THE SECOND DOOR OF THE BAPTISTERY AT FLORENCE

(PROBABLY JOEL AND HABAKKUK, RACHEL AND ESTHER)

98. AARON. BRONZE STATUETTE IN A NICHE OF THE SECOND DOOR OF THE BAPTISTERY AT FLORENCE (CF. NO. 45)

99. AARON. DETAIL OF NO. 98

100. ST JOHN THE BAPTIST. 1414. BRONZE. FLORENCE, OR SAN MICHELE

101. ST JOHN THE BAPTIST. DETAIL OF PLATE 100

102. ST MATTHEW. 1420. BRONZE. FLORENCE, OR SAN MICHELE

103. ST MATTHEW. DETAIL OF NO. 102

104-105. ST STEPHEN. 1427. BRONZE. FLORENCE, OR SAN MICHELE

106. ST STEPHEN. DETAIL OF NO. 104

107. THE BAPTISM OF CHRIST. 1424-27. BRONZE RELIEF ON THE FONT IN THE BAPTISTERY AT SIENA

108. ST JOHN THE BAPTIST BEFORE HEROD. 1424-27. BRONZE RELIEF ON THE FONT IN THE BAPTISTERY AT SIENA

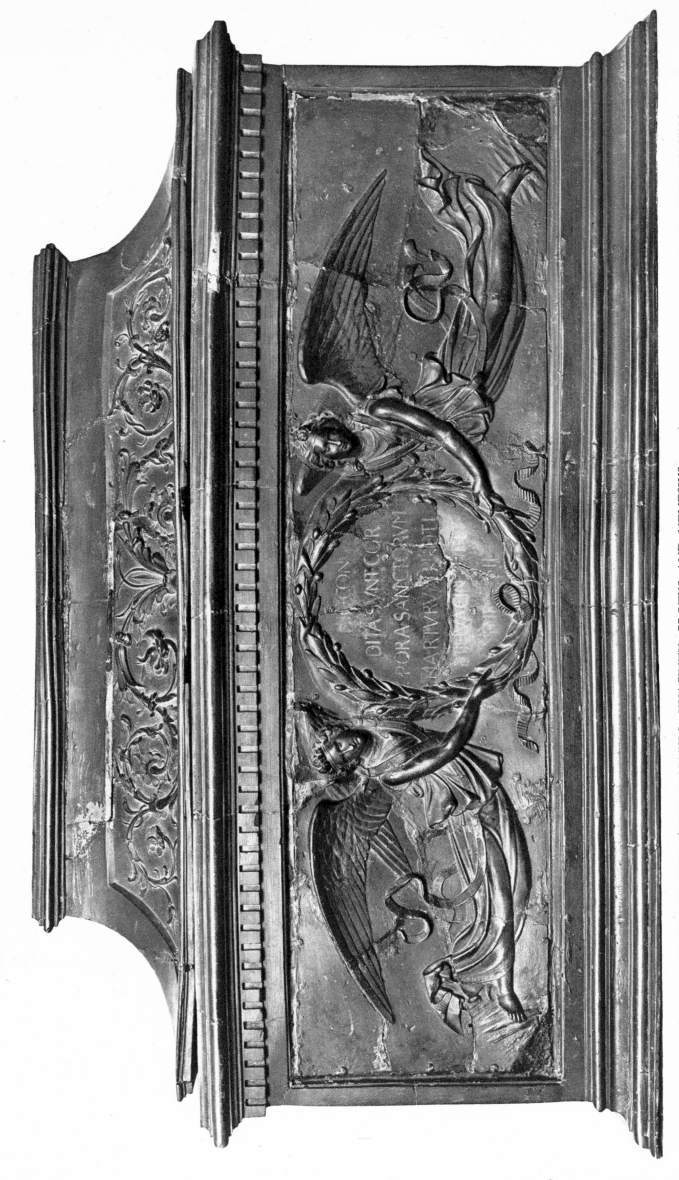

III. THE RELIQUARY OF THE THREE MARTYRS, HYACINTH, PROTUS AND NEMESIUS. 1428. WOOD WITH BRONZE RELIEFS. FLORENCE, BARGELLO

III-A. THE RELIQUARY OF THE THREE MARTYRS, AFTER RESTORATION OF THE BRONZE RELIEFS. COMPARE PLATE III

112–A. THE RELIQUARY OF ST ZENOBIUS. 1434–42. RIGHT SIDE VIEW. FLORENCE, CATHEDRAL

112-B. THE RELIQUARY OF ST ZENOBIUS. 1434-42. LEFT SIDE VIEW. FLORENCE, CATHEDRAL

112-C. THE RELIQUARY OF ST ZENOBIUS. 1434-42. WOOD WITH BRONZE RELIEFS. FLORENCE, CATHEDRAL, TRIBUNA DI SAN ZENOBI

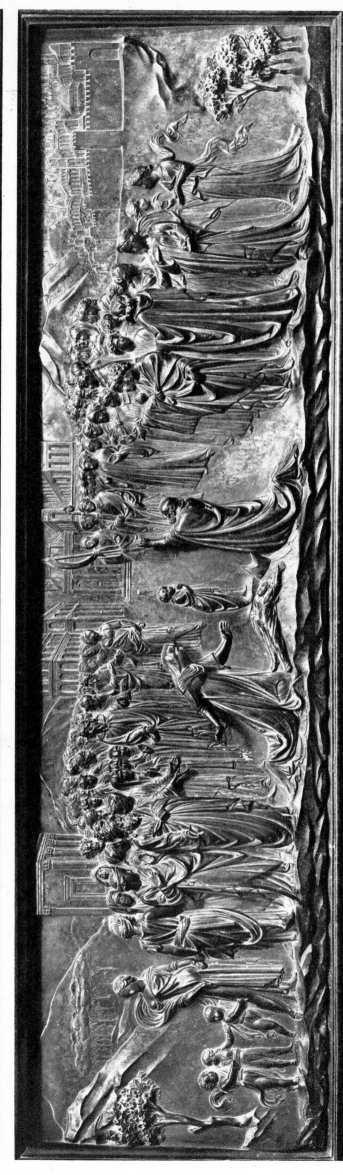

CAPVT
BEATI ZENOBII FL
ORENTINI EPISCOPI
INCVIVS HONOREM
HEC ARCA INSIGNIOR
NATV FABRICATA
FVIT

112-113. THE RELIQUARY OF ST ZENOBIUS. 1434-42. THE BRONZE RELIEFS ON FRONT AND BACK OF THE SHRINE. FLORENCE, CATHEDRAL, TRIBUNA DI SAN ZENOBI

114. GROUP OF WOMEN. DETAIL OF NO. 113

115. THE MOTHER OF THE DEAD CHILD. DETAIL OF NO. 113

116. THREE ANGELS. DETAIL OF NO. 112

118. **OUR LORD ENTHRONED.** 1450. BRONZE DOOR ON BENARDO ROSSELLINO'S TABERNACLE IN SANTA MARIA NUOVA, FLORENCE

119. OUR LORD. DETAIL OF NO. 118

120. THE VIRGIN AND CHILD. TERRACOTTA. (ASCRIBED TO GHIBERTI OR HIS WORKSHOP; ABOUT 1420.)
LONDON, VICTORIA AND ALBERT MUSEUM

121. **THE VIRGIN AND CHILD.** PAINTED AND GILT STUCCO (ATTRIBUTED TO GHIBERTI; ABOUT 1430)
WASHINGTON, NATIONAL GALLERY OF ART, KRESS COLLECTION

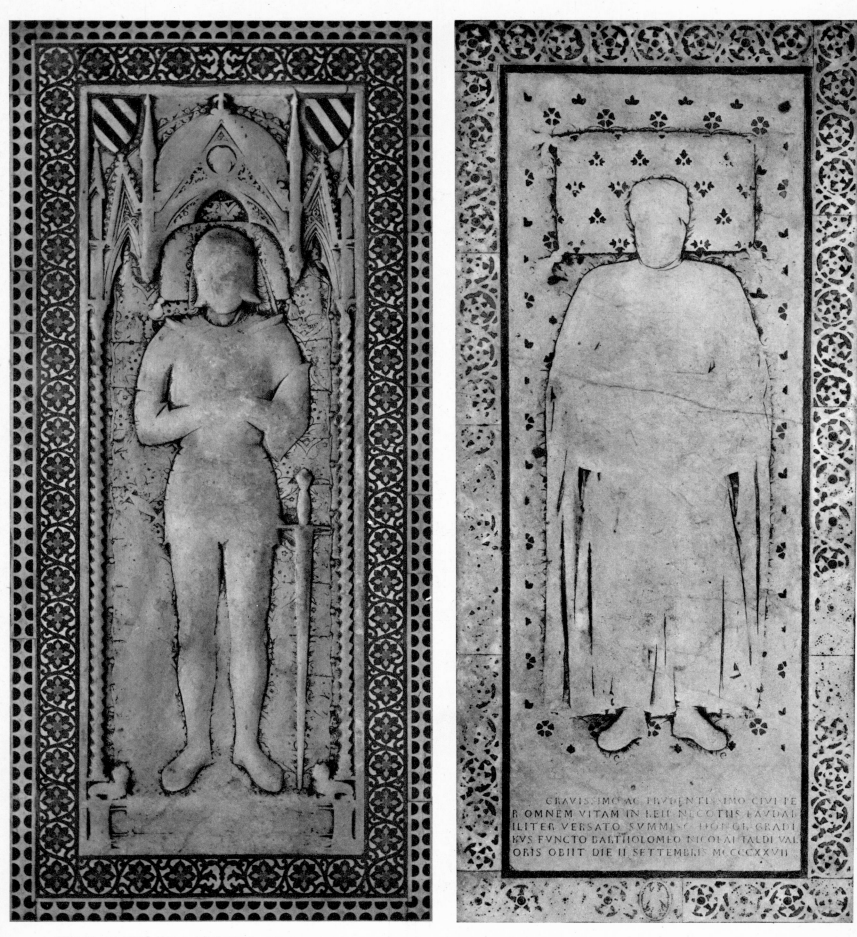

122–123. TOMB SLABS OF LODOVICO DEGLI OBIZZI AND BARTOLOMMEO VALORI. MARBLE, SCULPTURED BY FILIPPO DI CRISTOFANO FROM DESIGNS BY GHIBERTI. ABOUT 1427. FLORENCE, S. CROCE

124. TOMB SLAB OF THE MONK LEONARDO DATI. BRONZE. 1423–27.
FLORENCE, S. MARIA NOVELLA

125. **NATIVITY.** TERRACOTTA (ATTRIBUTED TO GHIBERTI ; ABOUT 1427)   DETROIT, MRS. EDSEL B. FORD

126. FRAME FOR FRA ANGELICO'S "ARTE DEI LINAIUOLI TRIPTYCH". 1432. WOOD AND MARBLE
EXECUTED BY JACOPO PAPERO AND JACOPO DI BARTOLO FROM DESIGNS BY GHIBERTI. FLORENCE, MUSEO DI SAN MARCO

127. VIRGIN AND CHILD IN A NICHE, WITH TEN ANGELS. STUCCO RELIEF.
(ATTRIBUTED TO GHIBERTI; ABOUT 1427-32) BERLIN, MUSEUM

128. FIVE STUDIES FOR EXECUTIONERS IN A SCOURGING OF CHRIST (CF. PLATE 14).
PEN AND BROWN INK, ABOUT 1415. VIENNA, ALBERTINA

129. ASSUMPTION OF THE VIRGIN. STAINED GLASS WINDOW, 1405. FLORENCE, CATHEDRAL

130. PRESENTATION IN THE TEMPLE. STAINED GLASS WINDOW, 1443. FLORENCE, CATHEDRAL

131. CHRIST ON THE MOUNT OF OLIVES. STAINED GLASS WINDOW, 1443. FLORENCE, CATHEDRAL

132. ASCENSION OF CHRIST. STAINED GLASS WINDOW, 1443. FLORENCE, CATHEDRAL

133–135. STAINED GLASS WINDOWS IN FLORENCE CATHEDRAL. 1441

136–138. STAINED GLASS WINDOWS IN FLORENCE CATHEDRAL. 1441–42

139–141. STAINED GLASS WINDOWS IN FLORENCE CATHEDRAL. 1442–43

CATALOGUE

GHIBERTI'S WORKS : NOTES ON THE PLATES
INCLUDING A LIST OF ATTRIBUTIONS

Fig. 12.   Christ.   Detail of pl. 132

The terms left and right are used from the standpoint of the spectator.

References to Ghiberti's Autobiography are to the English translation in the present volume, printed on pages 19-21.

The "Vita" by Vasari, to which the following notes often refer, is printed here on pages 22-25.

NOTES ON THE PLATES

THE WORK OF LORENZO GHIBERTI

Plate 1. GHIBERTI'S SELF-PORTRAIT, FROM HIS SECOND DOOR OF THE BAPTISTERY AT FLORENCE.

The diameter of the original, including the circular frame, is only about 5 in.; the reproduction is enlarged to more than twice the actual size in order to show the vigour of the modelling. The positon of the self-portrait on the second door can be seen on plate 45, where it occurs on the inner border of the left wing, between the third and fourth panel.

This portrait, which shows Ghiberti at the age of about 70, is actually a tiny bust, for it is worked in full relief. It is a realistic rendering of his countenance: the man who was the first artist to write his autobiography was also the first to leave a lifelike portrait of himself. In his days Italian art returned to naturalism for the first time since the Etruscan sculptors and the Roman portraitists.[1] Ghiberti's self-portrait, with its flabby cheeks, fleshy ears and nose, soft mouth, swollen eyelids, bald-headed, sober, clever and kind, strikes us as very modern because every detail is closely observed and reproduced; and we can read from it a character which we can understand without consideration of the period. It has nothing of the usual pose of the artist, but gives the features of a good craftsman: and it was as such that Ghiberti always regarded himself.

This self-portrait is mentioned by Vasari (¶19 and 29); and also by Filippo Baldinucci (who wrote Ghiberti's biography in 1681): "*The self-portrait of this great artist, made from life, can be seen in the centre of his magnificent bronze gate facing the Cathedral, next to that of Bartoluccio his stepfather, who is represented by a much older head than Lorenzo on the frame of the right-hand [?] wing, while that of Lorenzo is on the frame of the other wing.*" According to Pietro Cennini, who was the first to mention this self-portrait of Ghiberti in his *Memoriale* (written in Latin in 1475; published by Mancini in *Rivista d'Arte* VI, 1909, p. 221f.), the other head is a portrait of Ghiberti's son Vettorio (plate 79).

Plates 2 and 3. THE SACRIFICE OF ISAAC. THE TWO COMPETITION RELIEFS OF 1401 BY BRUNELLESCHI AND GHIBERTI. FLORENCE, MUSEO NAZIONALE DEL BARGELLO.

The two bronze plaques are of equal size (18 × 16 in.), but Brunelleschi's work is reproduced on a smaller scale because it does not properly belong among our plates and is shown only for the sake of comparison. The reproduction of the Ghiberti relief is a little more than half the size of the original.

The story of the competition is told at length by Ghiberti himself (¶3) and by Vasari (¶3 and 4). That Ghiberti "*enjoyed the help of Bartoluccio*" can well be believed, as the younger artist was only twenty-two at the time of the competition, and this relief looks more advanced than most of the panels of his first door. It is unfortunate that no work by Bartoluccio has yet been identified, and equally unfortunate that, apart from Brunelleschi's bronze, all the competition reliefs have disappeared, including that of Jacopo della Quercia. There is, however, a unique print from an engraving of the *Sacrifice of Isaac* in the Uffizi (Cat. No. 127; Hind 13) which is rather different from Brunelleschi's composition; it shows no relation to his style, but is built up naively in two planes, and might therefore be a last trace of one of the lost competition plaques.

Brunelleschi's relief was used as a decoration for the altar table in the old Sacristy of San Lorenzo, as Manetti, his first biographer, informs us ("*nel dossale dell'altare della Sagrestia*").

Ghiberti's relief was kept, Vasari tells us (¶4), "*all'udienza dell'Arte de' Mercatanti*", in the audience hall of the Guild of the Cloth-Merchants. It was gilded in 1407, before it was taken there.

Plates 4 and 5. GHIBERTI'S FIRST DOOR OF THE BAPTISTERY AT FLORENCE, WITH SCENES FROM THE NEW TESTAMENT.

One can best visualize the dimensions of the door by bearing in mind that the three figures above the architrave are slightly over life-size, about 7 ft. high. The door itself is 18 ft. 6 in. high and 12 ft. wide; without the frame (as shown in plate 5) 15 × 8 ft. 3 in. (the reproduction is reduced to one-fifteenth of the actual size). Each panel measures 16 × 16 in. There are 48 small heads, each about 4½ in. long. (See ¶4 and 5 of the Autobiography and ¶5-7 of Vasari).

Fig. 13. Andrea Pisano's Door of the Baptistery in Florence, 1329-38

This is the second door of the Baptistery.[2] The first was made by Andrea da Pontedera, also called Andrea Pisano, in 1329-38 (fig. 13). Ghiberti had to follow closely the form of Andrea's door, which consists of 28 panels in bronze, each scene in a quatrefoil frame. The door was ordered by the Guild of Cloth-Merchants (*l'Arte de' Mercatanti di Calimala*), and a special commission of the *Opera di San Giovanni*, the so-called *Ufficiali del Mosaico*, was appointed to control the progress of the work and all payments connected with it. An excerpt of their records was preserved by Carlo Strozzi,[3] and first appeared in print in Thomas Patch and Antonio Cocchi, *Porte di bronzo della chiesa di San Giovanni Battista*, Florence 1773; they were quoted and commented on by Giovanni Gaye, in his *Carteggio*, 1839, I, p. 106 f., reprinted by Eugène Muentz, in *Les Archives des Arts*, 1890, I, p. 15 f., and finally edited by Karl Frey, in 1911, in his *Vasari*, part I, p. 353 f., furnished with critical notes.

According to these records the commission was given to Ghiberti and his stepfather ("*a Lorenzo di Bartolo et a Bartolo di Michele, suo padre, orafi*"). The first records are dated the 3rd and 23rd of November, 1403. The work had to start on the 1st of December of that year. Three reliefs ("*tre compassi*") were to be executed every year and Ghiberti was allowed to use the help of assistants.

---

[1] This naturalistic movement began much earlier in the north; one might even assume that Netherlandish paintings sent to Italy encouraged the artists there to attempt a new approach to nature. If we were not a little tired of juxtapositions, we might place an illustration of Jan van Eyck's Cardinal Albergati of 1432 next to one of Ghiberti's self-portrait and reveal some surprising affinities.

[2] The numbering occasionally causes some confusion. The *second door* means in all documents the first door by Ghiberti. The three doors of the Florence Baptistery are:
(a) The south door with scenes from the Life of St John the Baptist by Andrea Pisano, 1329-38;
(b) The north door with scenes from the New Testament, by Ghiberti, 1403-24; his first door;
(c) The east door with scenes from the Old Testament, by Ghiberti, 1425-52; his second door.

[3] Senatore Carlo Strozzi (1587-1670), *Spoglio primo (secondo, terzo) delle scritture dell' Arte di Calimala, altrimente detta de' Mercatanti*, Firenze, Archivio di Stato (Uffizi).

Amongst these assistants were Donatello and Michelozzo, the painter Paolo di Dono, called Uccello, Bernardo Ciuffagni, who later became the assistant of Donatello, Maso di Cristofano, whom we know from the competition of 1401, and Giuliano di Ser Andrea, who in 1427 finished one of Ghiberti's Siena Font reliefs (pl. 108). Other assistants are also named in the records—Bandino di Stefano, Jacopo d'Antonio di Bologna, Antonio di Tommaso, Domenico di Giovanni, and many more—but their names do not convey anything. Vasari also mentions Filarete amongst the pupils. Brunelleschi probably helped, too, not only by "*polishing the reliefs*", as Vasari says, but also with the perspective of the architectural backgrounds. On the whole, it is rather surprising that Ghiberti with some twenty assistants took so many years to finish this door. However, after 1407, Bartolo, who a year before had married Ghiberti's stepmother, no longer worked in this *bottega*. The work was interrupted several times: in 1414 when Ghiberti was occupied with the *St John* (plate 100); in 1417, when the plague drove him and his assistants to Siena; when he was engaged on goldsmith's work (such as the two silver candlesticks which he designed for Or San Michele after his return to Florence in the same year, and the golden mitre for Pope Martin V in 1419); and in 1420, when the *St Matthew* was cast (plate 102).

The composition of the reliefs has been discussed in detail by August Schmarsow (*Ghibertis Kompositionsgesetze an der Nordtür des Florentiner Baptisteriums*, Leipzig 1899). Richard Krautheimer has attempted a chronology of the single reliefs (*Ghibertiana*, in *Burlington Magazine*, August 1937, p. 68 f.).

The stories begin in the lower left corner, run across the two wings of the door, and end in the upper right corner, an arrangement found also in the stained glass windows of the Cathedrals of Northern France,[4] but differing from that of Andrea Pisano's door or Ghiberti's own Old Testament door, where the stories begin in the upper left corner and end in the lower right-hand corner. This suggests that in the early fifteenth century French influence was felt not only in Verona and Rimini, but extended as far as Florence.

---

[4] A. Schmarsow, *Kompositionsgesetze frühgotischer Glasgemälde*, Leipzig, 1919.

Fig. 15. Baptism of Christ. Bronze plaque on Andrea Pisano's Baptistery Door

The door is signed by the artist. The signature, which begins below the self-portrait and continues on the right wing of the gate, reads OPVS LAVREN/TII FLORENTINI.

Ghiberti's first door was put in place and consecrated at Easter, 1424. A few months later the master and his assistants fled again before the plague, this time to Venice.

Here follow a few notes on individual plaques.

The bottom row (plate 5) shows *The Doctors of the Church*, the four eminent Christian writers who are so called in canon law on account of their learning and heroic sanctity. (See plates 36-38 and 40.)

The next row of four plaques shows *The four Evangelists*, characterized by their conventional symbols: St John by the eagle, St Matthew by the angel, St Luke by the ox, and St Mark by the winged lion (see plates 33-35 and 39). Michelangelo's *Jeremiah* is derived from Ghiberti's *St John*.

The third row from the bottom begins with the life of Christ according to the Gospels; it consists of twenty plaques. The first, the *Annunciation* (plate 6), is related in composition to a painting from Agnolo Gaddi's workshop (fig. 14) where the Madonna, holding her prayer-book and touching her heart with her right hand, stands in a similar small tabernacle. The *Baptism of Christ* (plate 17) closely resembles the corresponding plaque on Andrea Pisano's door (fig. 15). The *Storm on the Lake of Galilee* (plate 10) is based on Giotto's *Navicella*. For the *Scourging of Christ* (plate 14) a sketch has been preserved (plate 128). The last relief, the *Pentecost*, is one of the most interesting (plate 16).

Fig. 14. School of Agnolo Gaddi, c. 1390: Annunciation. Florence, Accademia

Fig. 16. Andrea da Firenze, c. 1366: Pentecost, fresco. Florence, S. Maria Novella, Spanish Chapel

Fig. 17. Fruit Garland from the "Ara Pacis Augustæ", c. A.D. 14.
Rome, Museo delle Terme

First, it contains in the upper centre a small Madonna relief which is so different from all the Madonnas attributed by various writers to Ghiberti that it becomes of great importance in the consideration of further attributions. Secondly, it contains curious oriental figures, probably taken from life. The man in the centre has his hair plaited. This composition is largely influenced by Andrea da Firenze's fresco in the Spanish Chapel (fig. 16), where an even more genuinely oriental-looking man with plaited hair stands at the door.

The beautiful foliage on the borders between the plaques is true to nature and at the same time very much in the spirit of the Renaissance—if we understand by it a revival of the conceptions of Roman sculptors. These garlands have interesting classical prototypes in those on the Ara Pacis (fig. 17). A further proof of Ghiberti's classicism are the small heads on the frame, of which we show three enlarged specimens (plates 42-44). One is in fact derived from an antique bust of Socrates (figs. 18-19).

Amongst the heads there is also a youthful self-portrait of Ghiberti (plate 41) at the age of about thirty-two.[5]

Figs. 18-19. Socrates. Antique marble in the Villa Albani, Rome;
and bronze head on Ghiberti's first Baptistery Door

Plate 45.   GHIBERTI'S SECOND DOOR OF THE BAPTISTERY AT FLORENCE, WITH SCENES FROM THE OLD TESTAMENT.

This door is of the same size as the first (plate 4), namely 15 ft. high and 8 ft. 3 in. wide (without the frame); the reproduction in plate 45 is about one-twentieth of the original. The ten plaques measure 31 × 31 in.[6]

(See ¶16 and 17 of the Autobiography and ¶19 to 23 of Vasari.)

---

[5] The two views of the head (in plate 41) are enlarged about 3 : 2. The reproductions of the single panels are about half the actual size (plates 6-16) two details (plates 19 and 20) are in original size, while another (plate 21) is half-size. The reproductions of the borders (plates 22-26) are reduced to half the actual size, the small reproductions of panels (plates 27-38) to a quarter.

[6] The single panels (plates 46, 51, 52, 55, 65, 67, 69, 71) are reproduced a little smaller than one-third of the original size. Of the details: 41, enlarged to about double size; 48, actual size; 56, two-thirds; 58, actual size; 59 and 60, two-thirds; 66, enlarged 3 : 2; 68, original size; 70, slightly enlarged; 72, two-thirds; 74, slightly enlarged; 75 and 76, about actual size. The heads are greatly enlarged—79 is more than double the original size. The reclining figures (plates 83-85), about two-thirds of actual size; the standing figures (86, 87) reproduced in about the same proportion, the others (as e.g. 89) almost original size.

The second door was also ordered by the *Arte di Calimala*, and the agreement was signed on the 2nd of January, 1425. The documents are extant and reprinted in the books named in my note on the first door; of these reprints, that in Karl Frey's *Vasari*, part I, Munich, 1911, pp. 357-364, is the most exact. Based on the documents is Heinrich Brockhaus's long article on the second door (*Forschungen über florentinische Kunstwerke*, Leipzig, 1902, pp. 3-50: *Die Paradies-Thür Lorenzo Ghibertis*). The style of the reliefs is analysed by August Schmarsow (*Gotik in der Renaissance*, Stuttgart, 1921, pp. 40-51).

The door bears Ghiberti's signature, below his self-portrait and the portrait of his son Vettorio; this inscription is mentioned by Vasari (¶29).

The *programme* for this door, i.e. the themes for the single reliefs, were worked out by Leonardo Bruni of Arezzo, who is best known for his *Life of Dante*. Bruni suggested 28 panels, twenty stories (as on Andrea Pisano's door and on Ghiberti's first door) and eight prophets; but Ghiberti did not follow Bruni's programme (see Frey, p. 358, and Brockhaus, plate II, and p.6).

Amongst Ghiberti's assistants are mentioned: Michelozzo; the master's two sons, Tommaso and Vettorio; Bernardo Cennini, who later on became the first printer in Florence; Benozzo Gozzoli, who was already twenty-four when he signed a three years' contract with Lorenzo and Vettorio Ghiberti, but whose datable paintings are of a much later period. The Anonimo Magliabechiano asserts that Luca della Robbia, Antonio and Bernardo Rossellino and Antonio Pollaiuolo (cf. note on plate 75) were also amongst Ghiberti's pupils and assistants.

In 1437, when the agreement with Ghiberti was renewed, three of the reliefs had been finished: *Cain and Abel* (plate 51); *Jacob and Esau* (plate 57); and *Moses* (plate 65); *Joseph* (plate 61) and *Solomon* (plate 71) were half-finished. How far the work on the other five panels[7] had proceeded in these twelve years we do not know; there is, however, a puzzling inscription on the top of Abraham's tent (plate 55) which may be read as 1436. By 1443 six panels were finished, which means that in another six years Ghiberti had completed only the two reliefs which were half-finished in 1437, and added one.

The framework was probably begun about 1430, but had had to be altered. In 1439 the casting of the frame was ordered again; with the help of three assistants it was finished in 1443. Bronze was bought in Bruges between 1440 and 1445. The small heads, probably begun in 1444, when Benozzo Gozzoli entered the workshop, had not yet been cast in 1448, but by 1447 everything else—apart from the outer frame—was finished and chased. Not until 1452 was the door completely finished, gilded and consecrated.

The whole work had taken twenty-seven years; but it was often interrupted. In 1425, right at the start, when Ghiberti was also working on his two reliefs for the Siena Font, he wrote to his friend Giovanni Turini: "*I have decided to do without any assistants and to remain master of my own workshop*"; two years later when he finished the Siena reliefs, he had at least three helpers; in 1437 he employed, in addition to Michelozzo and his son Vettorio, three *garzoni*; between 1444 and 1448 the share of these and other assistants was increasing and in the last years most of the work was probably done by Vettorio Ghiberti[7A] and Bernardo Cennini. While engaged on his second door, Ghiberti undertook many other commissions—the three tomb slabs, the two shrines of Saints, the *St Stephen* of Or San Michele, some goldsmith's work and many glass paintings; between 1438 and 1442 the work on the door was almost completely abandoned. The miracle about all this is that, with all these interruptions and all these many helpers, the completed door looks as if it were the fulfilment of a single inspiration and does not show any break of style.

Here follow a few notes on individual plaques.

Plate 46.

This, like some of the other reliefs, shows not one scene, but a number of scenes: *The Creation of Adam, the Creation of Eve, the Temptation and the Expulsion from Paradise.*

Plate 51.

Several scenes which can easily be identified from the text of the Bible. The group *Cain ploughing with a Yoke of Oxen*, so much praised by Vasari (¶20), is adapted from Andrea Pisano's Campanile relief, which is said to have been derived from a drawing by Giotto (figs. 20-21).

---

[7] There is documentary evidence that all ten reliefs and the twenty-four figures for the niches were cast but not chased as early as 1436: "4 *April. Historie* 10 e pezzi 24 di fregi delle porte di S. Giovanni gettati si cominciano a nettare per Lorenzo di Bartoluccio e un suo figliuolo e Michelozzo di Bartolommeo".

[7A] Art Bulletin, March 1948, p. 59, a document (published by R.G.Mather) dated Febr. 20, 1457 o.s. (= 1458): "*Vettorio di lorenzo ghiberti lavora per le porte di sangiovanni etc.*" After his father's death Vettorio made the bronze frame round Andrea Pisano's door.

Fig. 20. Andrea Pisano: Adam ploughing. 1337-42. Florence, Campanile.

Fig. 21. Ghiberti: Cain ploughing. Before 1437. Florence, Baptistery

Plate 62.

Vasari (¶20) speaks of *"a gold cup in Benjamin's sack"*; the Vulgate calls it a silver cup. Our caption follows Vasari.

One of the figures in this relief (cf. plate 63 and figs. 23-24) is influenced by a famous Giotto figure.

Plate 69. (Fig. 22.)

The relief lost some of its atmospheric mellowness by its recent cleaning since the hollows are no longer filled with black. But it must be admitted that all the reliefs now appear much closer to what Ghiberti intended us to see.

Plate 71.

This is the relief most improved by the cleaning; it is reproduced in its present state as frontispiece of this volume.

Plate 75.

Vasari, in his Life of Antonio and Piero Pollaiuolo, says: *"Their father ... put Antonio with the goldsmith Bartoluccio Ghiberti, then a famous master of the craft, and Piero with Andrea del Castagno, then the best painter in Florence. Antonio, being instructed by Bartoluccio, learnt to set jewels and prepare silver enamel work and was considered the most skilful workman with his tools that the art possessed. Thus Lorenzo Ghiberti, being then busy with the doors of S. Giovanni and happening to see Antonio's work, employed him as well as many other youths. Antonio, being set to work on one of the festoons which may still be seen there, made a quail so finely that it lacks nothing but the power of flight."* The same attribution is made by the Anonimo Magliabechiano in his note on Antonio Pollaiuolo.[8] As Pollaiuolo is not

[8] Ed. K. Frey, p. 81: *"Et anchora in sua gioventu lavora nelle porte d'essa chiesa con Lorenzo di Bartoluccio; et infra le altre cose fece nello stipito della porta di mezo una quaglia, molto delicatamente lavorata."*

Fig. 22. The Battle against the Philistines. Bronze relief, after cleaning (cf. plates 69 and 70)

Figs. 23-24.   Giotto: Ira. About 1306. Padua, Cappella dell' Arena.
Ghiberti: A brother of Joseph. About 1436. Florence, Baptistery

Fig. 25.   Detail from the Frieze of Ghiberti's second Baptistery Door. 1448-52.
(Perhaps by Antonio Pollaiuolo)

mentioned in the documents—unless he can be identified with the anonymous *garzone* who received a salary of 30 fiorini in 1448—it remains doubtful whether he ever worked with Ghiberti. Schorn and others identified Pollaiuolo's bird with the one shown here on plate 75 ; if this is more than a traditional attribution, the bird on the opposite side of the frame (fig. 25) should also be by Pollaiuolo.

Plate 79.   See note on plate 1, towards the end.

The twenty-four small heads or busts on Ghiberti's second door have a classical prototype—the *imagines clipeatae* (of which there is a famous example at Marbury Hall, Cheshire), and portrait heads on Roman silver plates (fig. 26—found long after Ghiberti's time, but the finest known piece) ; this type was not forgotten during the Middle Ages, and was used in the so-called St John salvers (fig. 27).

Plates 83-85.

There are altogether four of these reclining figures; the fourth is reproduced as plate 73F.

Plates 92-95.

Leonardo Bruni's *programme* suggested the following list of prophets : Samuel, Nathan, Elijah, Eliezer, Isaiah, Jeremiah, Ezekiel, Daniel. The names I have given here tentatively to Ghiberti's statuettes are based on a comparison with representations of the prophets in later Florentine art ; the Jeremiah for instance shows pronounced similarities to Michelangelo's picture of this prophet in the Sistine Chapel.

Plates 96-97.

Both figures are modelled on antique bronze statuettes.

Plate 98.

It is worth while comparing this statuette with the three over-life-size figures of Or San Michele (plates 100, 102, 104). The statuettes were modelled in 1436, whereas the large figures are of a much earlier date, the last dating from 1427. The prophet statuettes are indeed much more monumental, despite their small scale.

Figs. 26-27.   Roman silver plate with portrait bust. From Boscoreale, time of Augustus. Louvre.—St John salver, wood, about 1375. Nuremberg, Museum

Plate 100. ST JOHN THE BAPTIST. FLORENCE, OR SAN MICHELE. About 8 ft. high.

Baldinucci, who (in 1681) had access to documents now lost, namely Ghiberti's *zibaldone* or expense book, gives the best record of the statue: '*After.he had completed this work* [his first Baptistery door], *which earned him great renown, he was commissioned by the same Cloth Merchants' Guild to found a bronze statue of St John the Baptist for one of the niches of Or San Michele. Of this I find an original record by his own hand in a book entitled:* "*Journal of Lorenzo di Cione di Ser Buonaccorso, goldsmith of Florence, wherein I shall put down my business day by day, and so I will keep a record of all my things, beginning on the first day of May, 1403.*"
"*On the first day of December, 1414. Hereunder I will keep a record of whatsoever I shall spend on the cast of the figure of St John the Baptist. I have undertaken to cast it at my own expense: if it does not turn out well I shall be held to forfeit my expenses; if it succeeds the Guild of Calimala have agreed that the Consoli and Operai in office at the time shall use such discretion towards me as they would use towards another master whom they might commission with the cast. From this day forward I shall keep a record of all expenses incurred in the cast.*"
This makes it plain that, as it was to be an over-life-size statue, the Florentines, wishing to make certain of success, had again invited divers masters as they had already done for the door; and it was Lorenzo who cast it most admirably. In it he already began to display signs of the excellent modern style, having been one of the first to study ancient sculptures, Greek and Roman, of which he brought together such a rare collection . . . that at his death he left bronzes and marbles estimated at over fifteen hundred gold florins . . . Lorenzo then felt the desire to try himself at a mosaic, and in the same loggia of Or San Michele, just above the statue of St John the Baptist, he made the half-length figure of an apostle which can still be seen there to this day.'
Of this mosaic, which Vasari also mentions, no more than a slight trace is left (Vasari ¶8; Autobiography ¶6). The statue is signed and dated *on the hem of the robe*: LAVRENTIVS GHIBERTVS MCCCCXIV. On this and the following two statues see A. Schmarsow, *Statuen in Or San Michele*, in *Festschrift zu Ehren des Kunsthistorischen Instituts in Florenz*, Leipzig 1897.

Plate 102. ST MATTHEW. FLORENCE, OR SAN MICHELE. About 8 ft. 6 in. high.

Ordered by the Guild of Bankers and Money Changers (*Arte del Cambio*) in 1419; signed and dated on the hem of the robe: OPVS VNIVERSITATIS CANSORVM FLORENTIAE A.D. MCCCCXX; but not finished and set up until 1422.
(Autobiography ¶8; Vasari ¶10.)
Ghiberti employed several assistants in this work, amongst others Michelozzo, one of the best bronze founders of his time.
All the documents are extant and were carefully edited by Alfred Doren (*Italienische Forschungen*, Vol. I, pp. 1-58, Berlin, 1906); the most important parts already appear in Baldinucci's Ghiberti biography, from which I quote here a short extract.
"*26th August, 1419. The Signori of the Guild of Bankers and Money Changers, having assembled in the House of the said Guild to weigh all matters respecting the niche and the new figure of St Matthew which they desire shall be made of brass or bronze in the niche newly procured and acquired by the said Guild, have decided upon the allocation of the said niche and statue of St Matthew as described hereunder and have after diligent and secret scrutiny agreed by white and black ballots to commission Lorenzo di Bartoluccio of the Ward of S. Ambrogio, who is here present and who agrees, receives, and stipulates, for himself and his heirs; and they have accordingly made and drawn up the following contract and agreement.*
*Firstly, the said Lorenzo di Bartoluccio promises the aforenamed Consoli and four Arruoti and Operai by solemn agreement and stipulation to cast in bronze a statue of St Matthew which shall be at least as high as the Merchant Guild's statue of St John the Baptist or, if it will stand firmer, as much higher as appears necessary to the discretion of this Lorenzo. He shall cast the said statue in one piece or in two, that is in two pieces in all, namely the head in one piece and all the remainder in another; and the cost of the whole statue with its base, complete in the niche, shall not exceed two thousand five hundred libbre.
He further promises to work on the said statue, and to obtain the help of good and competent masters, who are proficient in such matters as this; and Lorenzo himself promises to work at the statue continuously during the agreed time, but for such intervals as shall be allowed and laid down by the Consoli of the Guild, present and future, and by the said four Arruoti and Operai; and he promises to complete, place in the niche, and hand over this statue within three years hence, reckoned from the sixteenth day of next July, and within such time and period save for legitimate hindrances recognized by the Consoli of the Guild then in office and by the Operai.
The same Lorenzo further told and assured the Consoli and the four Arruoti and Operai that as salary, remuneration and payment for his labour and for that of the said masters in placing the statue in the niche, he asked for, and was content with, the same amount as he had received from the Merchants' Guild as salary and remuneration for the labour on the statue of St John, which he had cast for that Guild, and that he asked for nothing else whatever from no person whatsoever.*

Fig. 28. Ghiberti: Tabernacle containing the St Matthew. Florence, Or San Michele
(The tabernacle executed by Jacopo di Corso and Giovanni di Niccolò; the Annunciation figures by Il Rosso.)

For their part the Consoli and Operai, in the name of the Guild, promised the said Lorenzo here present to provide whenever he asked for clay, iron, scaffolding, wax, brass, charcoal, timber and other things necessary and requisite for the statue, and to give him during the agreed time, day by day, such sums of money as shall be decided by the Consoli of the Guild, present or future, and by the four Operai. . . ."
The last stages of the work are best described in Baldinucci's words: "*After the said Guild had paid Ghiberti the sums necessary for the purchase of timber, iron, clay, cloth, wax, and human labour for the model and had instructed their treasurer Lapo di Biagio Vespucci to pay Giovanni di Bicci de' Medici two hundred and ninety-six gold fiorini for three thousand libbre of copper brought from Venice,[9] Ghiberti presented himself to the Guild on the sixteenth of July, 1421, to tell them that the cast had turned out faulty, and offered to have another cast made at his own expense; and for this purpose he was granted another thirty fiorini.[10] A sum of two hundred fiorini was, as provided for in the resolution, allotted for the final work on the said statue, namely for chasing and polishing it and placing it in the niche, and also for adorning the tabernacle with marbles both inside and outside.* (Fig. 28.) *They further resolved in May, 1422,[11] that two stonemasons, Jacopo di Corso and Giovanni di Niccolò, should build the tabernacle after a design by Ghiberti.*"

Plate 104. ST STEPHEN. FLORENCE, OR SAN MICHELE. About 8 ft. 6 in. high.

Ordered by the Guild of Wool Merchants (*Arte della Lana*) in 1427, finished in 1428. (Autobiography ¶14; Vasari ¶11).
The right hand held originally some object, probably a palm leaf.
A tempera painting on cambric linen in the Print Room of the Louvre, 27½ × 11½ in., of a Saint standing in a niche, has wrongly been connected with Ghiberti's *St Stephen* (H.Kauffmann, in *Berlin Jahrbuch*, 1929; Schlosser, fig. 84; Alinari, phot. No. 1420). Berenson attributes it to Rossello di Jacopo Franchi (*Drawings of the Florentine Painters*, 2nd edition, No. 2391-B).

---

[9] Documents of January 9, 1421, printed in Doren, l.c., p. 32f.
[10] Documents in Doren, l.c., p. 34.
[11] 2nd May; the original document printed in Doren, l.c., p. 46f.

Plate 107. BAPTISM OF CHRIST.

Without frame 25 × 24 in.

Plate 108.   ST JOHN THE BAPTIST BEFORE HEROD.

Without frame 27 × 23 in.

Two Reliefs on the Baptistery Font in Siena.

This font is decorated with six bronze reliefs, of which one is by Donatello, one by Jacopo della Quercia, two by Turini and two by Ghiberti. The documents were published by Milanesi, *Documenti per la storia dell'arte Senese*, II (1854), No. 61 and 85, and nine letters by Ghiberti, cp. 119-125 ; Gaye, *Carteggio inedito*, vol. I (1839), p. 104; Bacci, *Jacopo della Quercia* (1929), p. 96f.;—R.G.Mather, in *Art Bulletin*, March 1948, p.56 (on the whole identical with Gaye, p. 104). The two reliefs were commissioned in 1417, when Ghiberti went to Siena with two of his assistants; they were more or less finished in 1425, but were not gilded and delivered until 1427.

In a letter[12] dated April 16, 1425, and addressed to his friend Turini, Ghiberti says: *"The stories are nearly finished. Giuliano di Ser Andrea is engaged upon one, I upon the other . . You are anxious to assist me in chasing and polishing* (nettare) *one of these reliefs and you say it would give you pleasure."* It is probable that Turini really gave some help with the chasing; he even came to Florence in June, 1426.[13] This help must concern the *Baptism of Christ* (pl. 107), as the surface of the figures shows similarities with Turini's relief *St John the Baptist preaching*, whereas other parts, such as the cloud of angels (plate 109), belong to Ghiberti's finest achievements.[14] The other relief, *St John the Baptist before Herod*, of which Ghiberti himself says that it was executed by Giuliano di Ser Andrea, offers more than one problem. Even assuming that Giuliano worked from a *modello* by Ghiberti, the quality of the execution is in part astonishingly good: the ornament on the pedestal is at least as fine as that on the altar in the competition relief (plate 3) and some of the heads are extremely expressive. If we believe that most of this relief was indeed made by Giuliano,[15] some Madonna reliefs, optimistically ascribed to Ghiberti, should also be considered works of this assistant. (See in the list of attributions on p. 148 the Nos. 6-11, which may be by the same hand as No. 1).

(Autobiography ¶7; Vasari ¶9.)

Fig. 29. Ghiberti: The Reliquary of the three Martyrs, side view.
Florence, Museo Nazionale del Bargello

Plate 111. THE RELIQUARY OF THE THREE MARTYRS.
Florence, Museo Nazionale del Bargello.

23 in. high, 42 in. wide, 11½ in. deep.
The reproduction is about a quarter of the actual size.
Ordered by Cosimo de' Medici for Santa Maria degli Angeli, a convent in Florence, where at one time the *Linaiuoli Triptych* (plate 126) also was kept. This convent was secularized during the French Revolution; French soldiers broke the Reliquary into pieces which they sold for old metal. Fortunately most of the pieces were recovered and brought to the Florentine museum in 1814. Seven years later a restoration was attempted by the bronze sculptor Marco Cossini, but he was unable to

fit in all the bits of metal and filled in some of the gaps with stucco. Thanks to the initiative of Prof. Filippo Rossi of the Museo Nazionale, the Reliquary has now been properly restored (plate 111-A and fig. 29).[16] This recent restoration is the work of Bruno Bearzi.

For documents see Gaye, *Carteggio* I, p. 104; G.Gronau in *Rivista d'arte* V (1907), p. 120.

(Autobiography ¶10; Vasari ¶13.)

Plate 112 (A-C) and 113.   THE RELIQUARY OF ST ZENOBIUS
(called "Zanobi" in Florence). Florence Cathedral.

The front relief measures 25 × 75 in.; the back relief 20½ × 75 in. (Plate 113); the side reliefs are squares of 25 in. (Plates 112-A, 112-B).

The body of St Zenobius, who was bishop of Florence about A.D. 400, was found in 1330 in the Church of S. Reparata, the old Cathedral of the city. The head was taken out, covered with silver and put in a stone chest (*forziere*). In 1428 the *Opera del Duomo* decided that a new tomb for St Zenobius should be constructed, consisting of an altar table surmounting a bronze sarcophagus. In 1432 a competition was opened; Brunelleschi was commissioned to execute the altar and vault, Ghiberti the bronze sarcophagus.

The documents were collected by Poggi (*Il Duomo di Firenze*, 1909, p. 172f.), but some of them appeared in Gaye's *Carteggio* I (1839), p. 543, and in Cavaluzzi's *S. Maria del Fiore, storia documentata*. However, Ippolito della Nane, in his *Vita di S. Zanobi* (Florence, 1685) already made full use of the documents, and as this source has never been mentioned, I quote from it here:

'*As the veneration and the cult of S. Zanobi, the Protector and Defender of Florence and Highest Patron of the Church, became ever more popular, and as the people of Italy, and the Florentines in particular, emerged from the vulgarity and ignorance in which they had been left by the barbarians, they began to think of honouring the sacred relics in a worthier manner than they had done hitherto. Hence the Commune of Florence decided in March, 1408, to build a special sepulchre for the body of the Saint in a suitable place. After lengthy deliberations, the Operai of S. Maria del Fiore resolved in 1428 that this sepulchre should be built in their church, which by that time had been almost completed; and having consulted the most eminent theologians, painters, sculptors and others as to the best place for the said sepulchre, they decided to set it up in the centre chapel of the tribune. Their resolution on this matter reads as follows:*
"*In the chapel which faces the main door of the Baptistery and which shall be known by the name of S. Zanobi, a hollow altar shall be built, the corpse and bones of the said Saint being deposited underneath in a chest made of bronze and marble; upon this altar shall be placed a statue of the Saint, three and a half cubits high and made of the same material; the altar itself shall be surrounded by rails so that one may see, but neither touch nor remove, the sacred relics, which shall be translated thither in solemn procession.*"
Later they changed their plan, and decided to deposit the body in another chapel below the first, as is clear from the following resolution taken in 1438:
"*Resolved that the ark with the relics of S. Zanobi be deposited underneath the vault of the said chapel, in the centre of the side facing the choir; that the vault be made as flat as possible in order to give more space below; that a window be let into this vault which shall come partly under the upper altar and partly above the altar below; that the window be of the same length as the altar or a little less, about one cubit and a half wide, or a little less. This window shall be let in for two reasons, one to admit air to the vault, and the other to make it possible to see the lights that will be placed round the altar in honour of the Saint. The upper altar shall be of marble supported upon four columns, and underneath the marble altar, between the four columns, shall be placed the bronze chest commissioned from Lorenzo di Bartoluccio.*"
After noting various matters bearing upon the disposition of the altar, the document goes on:
"*The front of the tomb shall have no reliefs, but an inscription as well as a door that will allow of taking out and putting back the head of the Saint,*" *and a little further on:* "*for the lower chapel where the body of the Saint will be kept, lights shall be always lit and devotions maintained.*"
It follows that the said chest was to contain only the head of the Saint and not, as some have believed, his body; and this is confirmed by another resolution of the Opera, taken in 1440, which reads:
"*The bronze chest ordered for the head of S. Zanobi shall be inscribed on the back with the following words surrounded by a garland: CAPVT BEATI ZENOBII FLORENTINI EPISCOPI IN CVIVS HONOREM HEC ARCA INSIGNI ORNATV FABRICATA FVIT.*"[17]
And in this form it can still be seen at the present day.
The commission for the said chest was given in 1432 to Lorenzo di Bartolo, that is to Ghiberti, who was found to be the most experienced master in all the arts required for such a work. It was, however, stipulated that the chest was to be completed within forty-two months; and since Ghiberti did not complete it

---

[12] Printed in full on pages 16-17 above.

[13] Schlosser, p. 42. W. Lotz, *Der Taufbrunnen des Baptisteriums zu Siena*, Berlin 1948, p. 22.

[14] *Il Codice Magliabechiano*, ed. Karl Frey, 1892, p. 275: "*The* Baptism of Christ *on the Baptismal Font of Siena is for the greater part the work of an assistant, namely Turini's, who rather spoiled Ghiberti's design*".

[15] According to documents he was amongst the assistants working on Ghiberti's first Baptistery door since 1405. See Krautheimer, in *Burlington Magazine*, 1937, p. 75.

---

[16] *Mostra di Opere d'Arte trasportate a Firenze durante la Guerra*, Firenze, May 1947 (No. 66). It remains doubtful whether the relief which is supposed to have decorated the back of the reliquary is now lost or if there never was one—Ghiberti and Vasari mention only the front relief.

[17] The author of this inscription was Leonardo Bruni, who was also responsible for the *programme* of Ghiberti's second Baptistery door.

within that time, the commission was withdrawn.[18] *But as no one else could be found able to carry on the work with the perfection with which Ghiberti had begun it, it was given to him once more on April 18, 1439, with the stipulation that he should complete it within ten months from that date.*

How much they paid for this truly magnificent work I have not been able to ascertain. But I know that the Opera bought the Bronze from the Wool Merchants' Guild, who had it left over from the Statue of St Stephen, which they had set up at Or San Michele. One may perhaps accept the statement of a contemporary, or slightly later, account[19]*, which states that it cost one thousand three hundred and fourteen florins, but does not specify whether this covered only the artist's work or the entire cost.*

On the 26th of April, 1439, the relics were solemnly translated[20] *from the place where they had been deposited in 1330 to the chapel appointed for the purpose. For the descent into this chapel a staircase was ordered, which was to be perforated so as to admit the light. But the execution of this staircase was entrusted to Filippo di Ser Brunelleschi, who did not approve of such a design; hence it is now of a different shape.*

In the year 1590 the chest was gilded at the expense of Vittorio dell'Ancisa, a Chaplain of the same Church, who wished to shew his piety and devotion towards the Saint. The work was, however, carried out badly, and at present it is proposed to have the chest gilded afresh.'

On October 22, 1434, the bronze for the reliefs was bought in Venice; this probably means that at least Ghiberti's sketches in terracotta or wax were finished at this date. Ippolito della Nane's statement that some bronze, left over from the St Stephen statue, was bought from the *Arte della Lana* would mean that another quantity of bronze was bought in 1428 or a little later (cf. Poggi, doc. 898, dated 1428). The chest was finished on January 22, 1442, and the last payment to Ghiberti is dated August 30 of the same year. The side reliefs (plates 112A and B) are inferior in quality to the two larger reliefs (plates 112-113).
(Autobiography ¶15; Vasari ¶14.)
See Arnaldo Cocchi, *Ricognizioni e traslazioni delle reliquie di San Zanobi, vescovo di Firenze*, Florence 1900.—G. Poggi, *Il Duomo di Firenze* (1909) p. XCIV f.

Plate 118. CHRIST ENTHRONED. BRONZE DOOR OF BERNARDO ROSSELLINO'S TABERNACLE IN SANTA MARIA NUOVA (SANT' EGIDIO), FLORENCE.

11¾ × 8⅛ in. (Plate 118 shows the relief in about two-thirds of the actual size; plate 119 is about three times enlarged. The reproduction of this relief is not from the original but from a cast.)
The document was published by Giovanni Poggi, in *Miscellanea d'arte* I (1903), p. 106. The date is 1450.
Bernardo Rossellino is mentioned by the Anonimo Magliabechiano amongst Ghiberti's assistants on the second Baptistery door. If this is correct, it would afford a simple explanation of Ghiberti's collaboration with a sculptor who was by thirty years his junior.
This tabernacle was used for keeping the holy oil. (Fig. 30).

---

[18] March 9, 1437.

[19] A note by Buonaccorso, Ghiberti's grandson (Perkins, p. 147; Schlosser, p. 56).

[20] The head of St Zenobius was transferred to his new tomb under the auspices of Pope Eugenius IV, who at that time resided in Florence. Ghiberti's bronze chest was not completed until three years later.

Fig. 30. Bernardo Rossellino: Marble Tabernacle with Ghiberti's bronze sportello, 1450. Florence, Santa Maria Nuova

ATTRIBUTIONS

Ghiberti has had the very dubious advantage of having the list of his works, as given by him in his Autobiography, enlarged by some writers of great knowledge, authority, optimism and courage, who have attributed to him and his workshop a generous number of Madonna reliefs and statuettes and a few other sculptures. Schlosser accepted hesitatingly only one of these attributions (plate 125), Planiscig none. The first of these optimistic critics was Oswald Sirén, who ingeniously but unconvincingly started the fashion of Ghiberti attributions.[21] Wilhelm von Bode followed with a long essay on Ghiberti as the leading Florentine master of terracotta reliefs and statuettes[22] and gave his final view in the sixth edition of his Handbook of Italian Sculpture[23], in which eight of the sculptures in the Berlin Museum are ascribed to Ghiberti.[24] Oskar Wulff's article on Madonna reliefs attributed to Ghiberti several

other terracottas and stuccos.[25] Adolfo Venturi made additions to this list, though these are not Madonna reliefs. The result of all this was that the Berlin Museum had at one time at least a dozen works ascribed to Ghiberti or his workshop, the Victoria and Albert Museum had eight, others were thought to be in the Museums of Florence, Paris, New York, in several private collections and in art dealers' hands.

Most of these attributions are not taken very seriously nowadays. Four of them, for which there is a good case, I have reproduced here (plates 120, 121, 125, 127) and discussed briefly in the following notes. Of the others, as far as they are worth mentioning, I give a list and a few illustrations.

First, we must consider on what grounds the attributions of the Madonna reliefs are based. There is a passage in Ghiberti's Autobiography which gives scope for the guesswork of searchers: *"In order not to tire my readers, I shall refrain from mentioning other works I have produced. I know that such things will not be of particular interest. But I have assisted many painters, sculptors and masons to attain honour with their works by furnishing them with models in wax and clay. Painters in particular received sketch designs in quantities."* One may look around in vain for any paintings related to Ghiberti's designs of stained glass but there are numerous sculptures that are influenced by Ghiberti, and therefore were claimed as being his or from his workshop.

---

[21] *Due Madonne della Bottega del Ghiberti*, in *Rivista d'Arte*, 1907, p. 48f.—Also *Essentials in Art*, London, 1920, p. 138.

[22] *Lorenzo Ghiberti als führender Meister unter den Florentiner Tonbildnern*, in *Berlin Jahrbuch*, Vol. 35, 1914, p. 71f. Reprinted in his *Florentiner Bildhauer der Renaissance*, 1921, p. 73f. 1, of which there is also an English translation.

[23] *Die Italienische Plastik*, in *Handbücher der staatlichen Museen zu Berlin*, 1922.

[24] F. Schottmüller, in the second edition of the Renaissance Sculpture Catalogue of the Berlin Museum, accepts only one of Bode's attributions (plate 127), but has two new ones (figs. 36 and 38).

[25] *Ghibertis Entwicklung im Madonnenrelief* in *Amtliche Berichte der Berliner Museen* (Beiblatt zum Preussischen Jahrbuch, 1922), XLIII, pp. 91-103.

Fig. 31.   Detail of a Glass Window, designed by Ghiberti, 1442

Fig. 32.   Terracotta Relief. Johannesburg, Miss Heather Price

There exist indeed two Madonna representations by Ghiberti himself, and they should be taken as a basis: (1) the praying Madonna in the upper triangular space of the Pentecost relief (plate 16) of about 1420, and (2) a Madonna with a standing child which appears on one of the Florence Cathedral windows (plate 140 and fig. 31), designed by Ghiberti in 1442. The only Madonna relief I know which corresponds with this design is reproduced here (fig. 32). The crowned head turned towards the right, the head of the boy inclined in the same direction, his arm curved round the mother's chest, and many other similarities are apparent; nevertheless I should not go any further than to say that the relief is perhaps based on a model by Ghiberti. (According to Pope-Hennessy this relief is by the same hand as the figure of a standing Madonna in the Bargello.) The case for the other attributions, as given in the following list, is still weaker. All I have been able to do is to attempt a grouping of the works, which are definitely not by one hand.

(1) GIULIANO DI SER ANDREA (?): CRUCIFIXION, Victoria and Albert Museum, 5786—1859, catalogue of 1932: p. 15, pl. 9d. (reproduced here, fig. 33).
Closely related to Giuliano Fiorentino's *Crucifixion*[26] in Valencia Cathedral, c.1418 (cf. fig. 34).
Both reliefs are probably based on a lost composition by Ghiberti. The crowding of the figures in the London relief is similar to that in the *Herod* plaque in Siena (plate 108) and for this reason the London relief may be tentatively ascribed to Giuliano di Ser Andrea (fig. 33).

(2-5) MICHELE DA FIRENZE[27]
    (2) Berlin 129 (reproduced here, fig. 36).
    (3) Madonna Silten (Wulff,[28] illustr. 78).
    (4) Madonna Volpi (from Palazzo Davanzati in Florence, now in America; reproduced here fig. 35).
    (5) New York, Metropolitan Museum (reproduced here, fig. 37).

(6-11) THE MASTER OF THE TUCHER MADONNA. (THE WORK OF THIS ANONYMOUS MASTER SHOWS STRONG INFLUENCES OF GHIBERTI BUT ALSO OF JACOPO DELLA QUERCIA, LUCA DELLA ROBBIA AND OTHERS.)
    (6) Madonna formerly in the collection of Baron H. von Tucher, Vienna (Bode, illustr. 16, p. 55. Fabriczy[29] illustr. p. 72).
    (7) Berlin 7164 (reproduced here, fig. 38).
    (8) Detroit, Edsel B. Ford Collection (reproduced in W.R. Valentiner's *Donatello and Ghiberti*[30], illustr. 11).
    (9) The Huldschinsky Madonna (Bode, illustr. 43, p. 86).
    (10) Berlin, 134, p. 5.
    (11) Berlin 1566, p. 4.

(12-19) NANNI DI BARTOLO, CALLED IL ROSSO. (STRONGLY INFLUENCED BY GHIBERTI, DONATELLO AND JACOPO DELLA QUERCIA.)
    (12) Berlin 1562, p. 18.
    (13) The Aynard Madonna, Paris, Louvre, Cat. No. 1881 (illustr. Bode, fig. 42, p. 85).
    (14) The Rochester Madonna (Valentiner, illustr. 13; reproduced here, fig. 39).
    (15) Louvre (illustr. Bode, fig. 44, p. 87).
    (16) Victoria and Albert Museum 7574—1861, p. 14, pl. 8a.
    (17) Berlin 1991, p. 5.
    (18) Berlin 138, p. 18.
    (19) Detroit, Institute of Arts (Valentiner in *Art Quarterly* III, 1940, p. 182; reproduced here, fig. 43).

(20) MASTER OF THE MADONNA AT SAN MARTINO A PONTORME. Victoria and Albert Museum 8378—1863, p. 14, pl. 8b. (Ascribed by Siren to School of Ghiberti. Schottmüller, in *Berlin Catalogue*, under No. 128, p.24, thinks it might be by Michele da Firenze. Bode, p. 78, compares this and similar statuettes to a figure in Ghiberti's relief *Christ in the Temple*, reproduced here pl. 8 and fig. 41; it can be connected more easily with a figure in the *Calvary* relief, pl. 15 and fig. 40, or with Rosso's Madonna on the left above the *Matthew* Tabernacle, fig. 28. The London Madonna is reproduced here as fig. 42. The attribution as given in the heading is due to Ulrich Middeldorf (*Rivista d'Arte*, XX, 1938, p. 97.)

---

[26] A. Schmarsow, *Juliano Fiorentino*, Leipzig, 1911, p. 20—A.L.Mayer in *Bollettino d'Arte* II, 1922/23, p. 337f.—Also illustrated in Schubring's *Italienische Plastik des Quattrocento*, Berlin 1924, p. 25.—Here reproduced as fig. 34.
[27] Fiocco in *Dedalo* XII, 1932, p. 452; Maclagan, *Catalogue of Italian Sculpture in the Victoria and Albert Museum*, 1932, p. 13; Schottmüller, *Die Italienischen Bildwerke in Berlin*, Vol. I, 1933, p.23. (Schottmüller believes that some of the sculptures formerly given to the Modena master and others attributed to the Pelligrini master are works of Michele da Firenze.)
[28] *Ghiberti's Entwicklung im Madonnenrelief* in *Amtliche Berichte der Berliner Museen* XLIII, pp. 91-103.—Here, and in the other notes, "illustr." indicates that the work is reproduced in the article or book quoted; while "fig." refers to a reproduction in the present catalogue.

[29] Cornelius von Fabriczy, *Kritisches Verzeichnis toskanischer Holz- und Tonstatuen bis zum Beginn des Cinquecento* in *Berlin Jahrbuch* XXX, Beiheft, 1909, p. 1-88.
[30] A brilliant article in *The Art Quarterly* III, 1940, pp. 182-214, which did not, however, encourage me to extend my list of genuine Ghiberti sculptures.

The Crucifixion (after a lost relief by Ghiberti?)
Fig. 33.   Terracotta, by Giuliano di Ser Andrea (?)   Fig. 34.   Marble, by Giuliano Fiorentino
London, Victoria and Albert Museum   Valencia Cathedral

Fig. 35.   Madonna in a Niche, glazed terracotta. (Attributed to Ghiberti by Bode.) Formerly Florence, Palazzo Davanzati

Fig. 36.   Madonna under a Cupola, terracotta, painted and gilded. (Attributed to Ghiberti by Wulff and Schottmüller.) Berlin, Museum

Fig. 37.   Madonna in a Niche, terracotta, painted and gilded. (Attributed to Ghiberti by Bode and Valentiner.) New York, Metropolitan Museum

Fig. 38. Madonna and Child, terracotta.
(Attributed to Ghiberti by Schottmüller.)
Berlin, Museum

Fig. 39. Madonna and Child, terracotta. (Attributed to Ghiberti by
Valentiner.) Rochester, U.S.A., Memorial Art Gallery

Fig. 40.   The Virgin. Detail from plate 15.
By Ghiberti

Fig. 41.   The Virgin. Detail from plate 8.
By Ghiberti

Fig. 42.   The Virgin Annunciate, terracotta.
London, Victoria and Albert Museum

(21-22) MICHELOZZO
>   (21) Berlin 1940, p. 6.
>   (22) Berlin 73, p. 17.

(23-28) SCHOOL OF LUCA DELLA ROBBIA
>   (23) Berlin 130, p. 29.
>   (24) Berlin 132, p. 32.
>   (25) Berlin 7181, p. 33.
>   (26) Amsterdam, Rijksmuseum, Lanz Collection.
>   (27) Florence, Bargello.
>   (28) Victoria and Albert Museum. 33—1910, p. 15, pl. 10c.
>   (This is a very popular composition, of which many other
>   versions are extant, executed in different periods and by
>   different, but inferior hands; some could be ascribed to
>   Rosso, e.g. the London stucco, others were produced in
>   Bologna and show strong influence of Jacopo della
>   Quercia.)
>   (28A) Victoria and Albert Museum, 1354—1901, p. 15, pl.
>   10b. (By an eclectic artist who was influenced not so much
>   by Ghiberti as by Luca della Robbia. It should be of about
>   the same date as Luca's bronze reliefs on the door of
>   Florence Cathedral and the leather relief in Berlin 2414.)

(29) FRANCESCO DI VALDAMBRINO
Berlin 198, 199. (Bode: School of Ghiberti; Bacci and Schottmüller:
School of Jacopo della Quercia; Carlo L. Ragghianti: Valdambrino.[31])

---

[31] In *La Critica d'Arte*, XVI-XVIII, 1938, p. 140.—The two statuettes are of
walnut wood.

Fig. 43.   Madonna and Child, painted terracotta. (Attributed to Ghiberti
by Valentiner.) Detroit, Institute of Arts

Fig. 44. Small Bronze Statuette.
(Attributed to Ghiberti by Bode and
Schubring.) Berlin, Museum

(30)   IMPRUNETA NEAR FLORENCE: CRUCIFIX[32].

(31)   BERLIN, Inv. No. 2602. Bode's Catalogue of 1914, No. 18
(reproduced here, fig. 44).
Very weak; perhaps by the same imitator as the *Impruneta Crucifix*.

(32)   CASTEL DI SANGRO, IN THE ABRUZZI: TWO RELIEFS.[33]
These reliefs were found together with stuccos of Ghiberti's first
Baptistery door; they represent *Christ in the Temple* and *The Flight into
Egypt*. I know these two reliefs only from old photographs, but cannot
agree that they might be unused sketches by Ghiberti; they appear to be
by some much later, manneristic sculptor. Schottmüller, in the Berlin
Catalogue of 1933, p. 33, gives a list of early Ghiberti imitations and
says: "*His compositions were repeatedly copied, even in the fifteenth century,
either as a whole or in combination with motifs borrowed from elsewhere. Such
imitations are the Paliotto in the Duomo of Teramo by Niccolò di Guadia-
grele, reliefs in Castel di Sangro, Casa Patini, in Sulmona, and some others.*"
(See also Adolfo Venturi, *Storia dell' Arte Italiana*, vol. VI, p. 176-178.
with literature.)

(33)   ATTRIBUTIONS BY ADOLFO VENTURI IN HIS STORIA
DELL'ARTE ITALIANA[34]:
Illustr. 73, Or San Michele, St James; illustr. 74, Beheading of St James,
relief underneath the Or San Michele statue; illustrs. 94 and 95, Città di
Castello, Museo Civico, two silver statuettes from a reliquary. (The
St James is by Ciuffagni, who assisted Ghiberti with his first Baptistery
door; the two silver figures are similar in style to the two half-figures of
Prophets which Brunelleschi contributed in 1404, or a little later, to the
Silver Altar of Pistoia; but they are by some imitative craftsman.)

---

[32] Richard Krautheimer in the *Burlington Magazine* 1937, p.76f., pl.IIIc.
[33] Reymond, *Rilievi di Castel di Sangro*, in *L'Arte* V; cf. de Nicola in *L'Arte* XI, 1908.
—Balzano, *L'Arte Abruzzese*, in *L'Arte* IV, 1901 and V, 1902.
[34] Vol. VI, *La scultura del Quattrocento*, Milan 1908.

This list, though long, is not complete. The number of sculptures, representing almost every style of Florence and Northern Italy in the early Quattrocento, that have been attributed to Ghiberti during the last forty years, is amazing; the more so as Ghiberti's authentic work is of a very consistent character, which developed from the Competition Relief to the Zanobi Reliquary.

I have, however, little hope that my classification will be readily accepted. I have grouped these terracottas and stuccos according to their type, irrespective of whether they are originals or later repetitions. The hundreds of workshops in Florence, Siena, Bologna, Verona, and elsewhere, must have turned out and sold terracottas and stuccos of this kind by the score, and this from stock models; and just as in our own days people who buy a piece of furniture or printed silk will care only whether it is pretty, but not whether it is made from an original design or from whose design, so the Italians of the Quattrocento were good customers for this pleasing and eclectic output. Good sculpture was ordered too, but as we can see from the Ghiberti documents, it was very expensive and one had to wait many years before the artist finished it. Renaissance Florence was full of sculpture; but even in those days sculpture of the highest quality was scarce.

FROM GHIBERTI'S WORKSHOP

Plate 120. VIRGIN AND CHILD, TERRACOTTA, WITH TRACES OF PIGMENTATION AND GILDING. 29 in. high. (The reproduction is about one-third of the actual size.) London, Victoria and Albert Museum, 7573—1861.

Ascribed to Ghiberti by Bode, Wulff and Valentiner; rejected by Schlosser, Planiscig and Venturi.[35] This group shows a certain relationship to some terracottas which I ascribe to the Master of the Tucher Madonna[36], but is so much better in quality that I am inclined to accept it as one of the very few terracottas which were probably made under the master's own eyes and formed the starting point for the numerous variations produced in Florentine shops.

Plate 121. VIRGIN AND CHILD, STUCCO, PAINTED AND GILDED. 40 in. high, 22¾ in. wide. (The reproduction is little less than one-third of the original size.) Washington, National Gallery of Art, Kress Collection.[37]

The inscription on the base reads: AVE MARIA GRATIA PLEN. Ascribed to Ghiberti by Bode and others. The relief shows resemblances to some terracottas grouped here under the name of Nanni di Bartolo il Rosso.[38] The composition, though not the style, is related to the so-called *Madonna with the frightened Child*, of which there are versions in the Bargello at Florence, and in the Berlin Museum (Cat. No. 142, p. 28), variously ascribed to the schools of Jacopo della Quercia and of Luca della Robbia. The much superior quality of this relief, however, permits the attribution to a leading master. (Bode, in *Berlin Jahrbuch* XXXV, 1914, p. 80; Richard Krautheimer, *Terracotta Madonnas*, in *Parnassus*, Dec. 1936, p. 5. But see also the references in the Berlin Catalogue by F. Schottmüller, 1933, under No. 1562, p. 18.)

Plates 122-124. THREE TOMB SLABS. Florence, Santa Croce and Santa Maria Novella.

The tomb slab for Leonardo Dati (pl. 124) is mentioned in Ghiberti's Autobiography (¶9). Vasari (¶12) mentions also the other two tombs.[39] Leonardo Dati died in 1423, Lodovico degli Obizzi in 1424, Bartolommeo Valori in 1427. Ghiberti's tax return of 1427 (Gaye I, p. 105) gives evidence that in that year 10 florins were still due to him for the Dati tomb and 6 florins for the two others.[40] This suggests that all three were finished at about the same time.

The Obizzi tomb slab was executed from Ghiberti's design by the stonemason Filippo di Cristofano, and so perhaps was the Valori tomb slab. Even the Dati monument, which Ghiberti lists amongst his own works, can only be considered a workshop production; Giuliano di Ser Andrea may have had a share in it. The three tomb slabs are badly damaged; the bronze is naturally in a better state of preservation than the two marble reliefs, which are now almost flat.

Plate 125. NATIVITY. TERRACOTTA RELIEF WITH TRACES OF GILDING. 18¼ in. × 14 in. Detroit, Mrs. Edsel Ford.[41]

This is the only terracotta attributed to Ghiberti which Schlosser[42] thought worthy of consideration. The relief shows certain affinities to the plaques of the Siena font; the reclining Madonna recalls the St Elizabeth in Turini's *Birth of St John*, while the angels and trees are similar to some parts of Ghiberti's *Baptism* and the draperies are not unlike those in *The Baptist before Herod* by Ghiberti and Giuliano di Ser Andrea. It is difficult to accept this relief as a work by his own hand, but it can be regarded as coming from his workshop. One of three glazed terracotta reliefs in the Victoria and Albert Museum (7613—1861), *Adam and Eve*, is in parts almost identical with this one; the other two are more Sienese in character, though evidently by the same hand. These three reliefs were attributed at one time, with very little reason, to Ghiberti,[43] together with another glazed terracotta relief of the *Creation of Eve* (from the same series), in the Museo dell' Opera del Duomo, Florence.[44]

Plate 126. FRAME FOR FRA ANGELICO'S 'LINAIUOLI TRIPTYCH'. 17 ft. high, 8 ft. 10 in. wide. Florence, San Marco.

The *Arte de' Linaiuoli*, the Guild of Linen-manufacturers, ordered the painting from Fra Angelico in 1432, the frame from Ghiberti[45] in 1433. The frame was executed from Ghiberti's design by assistants in his workshop: Jacopo di Piero, called Papero, Simone di Nanni from Fiesole, and Jacopo di Bartolo[46], stonemasons and woodworkers. The triptych was originally in the Guild-House of the Linaiuoli, later in the Convent of Santa Maria degli Angeli in Florence; from 1777 to 1911 the picture was in the Uffizi and the frame in San Marco.

Plate 127. VIRGIN AND CHILD, IN A GOTHIC NICHE, BEFORE A CURTAIN, SURROUNDED BY ANGELS. Stucco, with traces of paint and gilding. 6¾ in. × 5⅛ in. Reproduced in original size. Berlin, Museum No. 1761.

The relief is in a gilded stucco frame, which is not reproduced here, forming a small tabernacle in the early Renaissance style. Probably a cast from a wax model for silversmith's work; badly preserved, broken in many places, parts chipped off, four heads missing; stylistically related to the Baptism relief in Siena (pl. 107) but even more closely to Turini's *sportello* on the Baptistery font in Siena. Attributed to Ghiberti by Bode and Schottmüller.

[35] Adolfo Venturi, *The Madonna*, London, n.d., p. 28: "*The Master of the Pellegrini Chapel*".

[36] See the list of attributions above, No. 6-11.

[37] Supposed to come from the church of Santo Spirito in Florence. From the collection Dr Eduard Simon, Berlin, and Clarence H. Mackay, Roslyn, Long Island.

[38] See the list of attributions above, No. 12-17.

[39] See H. Brockhaus in *Jahresbericht des kunsthistorischen Instituts in Florenz*, 1905-06; *Kunstchronik*, N.F. XVIII, 1906, p. 222.

[40] *Resto davere da frati di S.M. Novella fior. 10 della sepoltura chio feci pel generale. L'opera di S. Croce . . . fior. 6.*

[41] W.R.Valentiner, Catalogue of the Eighteenth Loan Exhibition of Old Masters, Detroit 1938, No. 23.

[42] Schlosser, *Ghiberti*, Basel 1941, p. 120.

[43] Wilhelm von Bode, *Ghibertis Versuche, seine Tonbildwerke zu glasieren*, in *Berlin Jahrbuch* XLII, 1921, p. 51f.

[44] Paul Schubring, in *Moderner Cicerone, Florenz* II, 3rd edition, 1925, p. 135: "*School of Ghiberti*".

[45] Michelangelo Gualandi, *Memorie originali italiane*, IV, Bologna 1843, pp. 109-111.— F. Schottmüller, *Fra Angelico*, Klassiker der Kunst, 2nd ed., 1924, pl. 36.—Poggi in *Italienische Forschungen* I, 1906, p. 37, note 3.—Milanesi, *Vasari* II, 1878, p. 514, note 2.

[46] The first, mentioned in 1422 as in Ghiberti's *bottega*, the second in 1427. Jacopo di Bartolo from Settignano, mentioned as early as 1407 as Ghiberti's *garzone*, is named again in the master's tax return of 1427. (Gaye, *Carteggio*, I, p. 105; Brockhaus, *Forschungen*, p. 46: Doren, in *Italienische Forschungen*, I, p. 36: K. Frey, *Vasari*, I, p. 356.)

GHIBERTI AS A DRAUGHTSMAN

Plate 128. DRAWING FOR 'THE SCOURGING OF CHRIST'
(pl. 14). 8½ × 6½ in.; reproduced in original size. Vienna, Albertina
(Cat. III, No. 8).

Accepted as by Ghiberti's own hand by Stix,[47] Panofsky,[48] Schlosser,[49]
and Popham.[50] There is, however, no authenticated Ghiberti drawing
with which to compare it.[51]

Plates 129-141. DESIGNS FOR STAINED GLASS WINDOWS
IN THE DUOMO AT FLORENCE.

The designs are mentioned in the Autobiography (¶20), but Ghiberti's
list is far shorter than that which we can compile from the documents.
Vasari (¶26) is not enlightening on this point. The documents were
published by Poggi.[52] The windows have been discussed by several
modern writers[53] and by Baldinucci, who made use of some documents,
but unfortunately only of those that do not refer to Ghiberti's cartoons.
Of the twenty-six windows in Florence Cathedral made from designs
by Ghiberti (the others are by Donatello, Castagno, Uccello, and by
glass painters of no renown), I have reproduced here just one half.
The remaining thirteen are either too much restored, as for instance
the two small *occhi* on the left and right of the *Assumption of the Virgin*,
or were too difficult to photograph. The four round windows are
reproduced here as they were before the cleaning, but the nine narrow
ones appear here for the first time in their clean state.

"I cannot recommend," says Burckhardt in his *Cicerone*, *"the examination of
the stained glass windows, as this is detrimental to the eye. One will do far better
to keep one's sight unimpaired for the study of the frescoes. But as there are many
important specimens of the art of the glass painter, I cannot ignore those works
completely; one should not, however, expect here any penetrating studies on
the subject."*

---

[47] *Albertina Facsimiles*, N.F. II, 1925, p. 35 (edited by J.Meder).
[48] *Das erste Blatt aus dem 'Libro' Giorgio Vasaris*, in *Staedel Jahrbuch* VI, 1930. p. 31.
[49] *Ghiberti*, p. 100, pl. 29.
[50] *Catalogue of the Albertina Exhibition*, London 1948, No. 11.
[51] How little we know about Ghiberti as a draughtsman is apparent from the fact
that a very different and still weaker drawing in the Louvre (see our note on plate 104,
p. 145) has been ascribed to him because it shows some likeness to his St Stephen at
Or San Michele; and this impossible attribution was readily accepted. The attribution
of the Albertina drawing is also far from being certain and I suspect that this is only
an imitation; perhaps by Parri Spinelli (1387-1453), whom Vasari mentions amongst
Ghiberti's assistants on the first door. There is a drawing in Bayonne (Berenson
1837-A), also ascribed to Parri Spinelli, which could as easily be connected with
Ghiberti's relief *Christ on the Lake of Galilee* (plate 10) as it is now with Giotto's
Navicella. 'Parri designed excellently,' says Vasari, 'in my *Libro* there are some
sheets of his beautifully drawn with the pen.' However, to attribute the Albertina
drawing to Parri Spinelli would be as speculative as to attribute it to Ghiberti.
[52] Giovanni Poggi, *Il Duomo di Firenze*, 1909, pp. LXXVIII-XC and pp. 85-171.
[53] H.Semper, *Die farbigen Glasscheiben im Dom zu Florenz*, in *Mitteilungen der K.K.
Zentralkommission*, Vienna 1872.—A.Marquand, *The Windows in the Cathedral of
Florence*, in *American Journal of Archaeology*, 1900, pp. 192f., with illustrations.—
H.Van Straelen, *Studien zur florentiner Glasmalerei*, Wattenscheid 1938.—Arthur Lane,
Florentine Painted Glass and the Practice of Design, in *Burlington Magazine* 1949, p. 43f.

Plate 129. ASSUMPTION OF THE VIRGIN.

Schlosser (pl. 92) dates this window from 1405 (Poggi, Doc. 517, 520),
but the documents refer to a cartoon by Pieri, which was probably
replaced at a later time by one of Ghiberti; the date is doubtful and one
would expect it to be 1432 as for the side windows.

This window design is mentioned by Ghiberti in his Autobiography
(¶20) and is certainly by him; only the early date, given to it by
Schlosser (whom I followed inadvertently in my caption of pl. 129)
is not acceptable.

Plate 130. PRESENTATION IN THE TEMPLE.
Poggi, Doc. 756: 1443. (Autobiography ¶ 20.)

Plate 131. CHRIST ON THE MOUNT OF OLIVES.
Poggi, Doc. 752: 1443. (Autobiography ¶20.)

Plate 132. ASCENSION OF CHRIST.
Poggi, Doc. 751: 1443. (Autobiography ¶ 20.)

Plate 133. ST BARNABAS
Poggi, Doc. 657, 677: 1441-42.

Plate 134. ST THOMAS.
Poggi, Doc. 657, 660: 1441-42.

Plate 135. ST PAUL.
Poggi, Doc. 654, 656 (605, 615, 622): 1441.

Plate 136. ST MATTHEW.
Poggi, Doc. 657, 658, 670: 1441-42.

Plate 137. ST JOHN THE EVANGELIST.
Poggi, Doc. 667, 671 (694): 1442.

Plate 138. ST STEPHEN.
Poggi, Doc. (659) 664: 1442.

Plate 139. ST PETER.
Poggi, Doc. (636) 655, 637: 1442.

Plate 140. MADONNA AND CHILD, WITH ST JAMES THE LESS AND
ST PHILIP.
Poggi, Doc. (659) 674; 1442.

Plate 141. ST ANTHONY
Poggi, Doc. (659) 702, 667: 1442-43.

INDEX OF PLACES

PLATES

The Baptistery in Florence